Pear Press
P.O. Box 70525
Seattle, WA 98127-0525
U.S.A.

This book may be purchased for educational, business, or sales promotional use.
For information, please visit www.pearpress.com.

FIRST EDITION

Library of Congress Cataloging-in-Publication has been applied for

ISBN-13: 978-0-9832633-6-4

Designed by Nick Johnson/Cima Creative

Printed in China

10 9 8 7 6 5 4 3 2 1

Pear
Press

ZERO *to* FIVE

70 Essential Parenting Tips Based on Science

(and What I've Learned So Far)

TRACY CUTCHLOW

Photos by Betty Udesen

Prepare

Love

Talk

Sleep, eat & potty

Play

Connect

Discipline

Move

Slow down

All of the photos are by Betty, except this one that Benjamin Benschneider made. Thanks, Ben!

About Tracy

I'm a former journalist at the Seattle Times, editor of the bestselling books Brain Rules and Brain Rules for Baby, and mom to one precocious 2-year-old. I like to think I'm a recovering perfectionist, but I still do way too much research on every little thing. I'm a city girl who loves to be outdoors. I'm staying home with baby, mostly, until either of us decides to renegotiate our contract. I live in Seattle with my husband, Luke Timmerman.

About Betty

Moments are special, don't you agree? My role is to anticipate fleeting glances, nuanced toe-curls and moist eyes that tell stories. I began using cameras in grade school, and I never stopped. Visual storytelling has taken me to Africa, Indonesia, Central and South America, and Israel. It also has deeply immersed me in the community of Seattle, where I worked for two-and-a-half decades as a staff photographer at the Seattle Times before leaving to pursue independent projects. I live in Seattle with my husband, Benjamin Benschneider (also a photographer) and three very nice cats.

We parents have questions.
Lots of questions.

Use this age key to jump to pages relevant to your child.

At least, I do. My husband and I had our first baby in our mid-30s, after months of "should we or shouldn't we?" We'd spent about fifteen minutes around newborns before that point. Like many expecting couples, our preparation consisted of birth-education classes. And research on diapers, clothing, and gear. (As avid cyclists, we had a balance bike picked out as early as a baby swing.) These weren't much help in how to raise a baby. Unlike many expecting couples, I'd edited the childhood brain-development book *Brain Rules for Baby*. Very handy! But, of course, no book can match the experience of *having a baby* right there in your arms, crying or cooing. We had questions then, and we have questions now.

Every parent I've come across has had challenges. The themes are similar, even if the particulars differ: Doing our best for baby during pregnancy, even when we don't want to. (Giving up wine or coffee comes to mind.) Sleep. Comforting baby. Feeding baby. Sleep. Getting out of the house. Getting a break. Keeping baby intellectually stimulated. Keeping up with friendships. Sleep. Digital devices. Discipline. Sleep.

My husband and I are certainly no different. Our baby surprises us, delights us, concerns us, and frustrates us. When she stumps us, I go looking for answers.

I ask friends. I talk with my mom. I search online, as my husband rolls his eyes. I like to consider all the options! But soon I'm buried in opposing opinions ("Best thing I ever tried"; "Didn't work for me AT ALL"), vague parenting articles, and irrelevant forum comments.

Then I'll flip through the many brain-development and parenting books on my shelf, accumulated while editing *Brain Rules for Baby* or writing this book. I pore through studies, staring at sentences like "Briefly, trajectory methodology uses all available developmental data points and assigns individuals to trajectories

≫

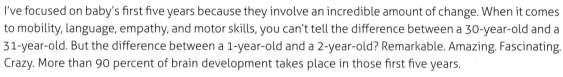

«

based on a posterior probability rule." All are filled with what seems, post-baby, like a very large amount of very small type.

And I think: it would be nice to have one inviting, just-tell-me-what-to-do, open-to-any-page collection of parenting's best practices, based on what the research says.

This is that book. The wonderful images were captured by photojournalist Betty Udesen. We met in 2001, when we worked together on multimedia stories for the *Seattle Times*. I asked her if she'd work with me on this book, and I feel very fortunate that she said yes.

Where do I get off writing a parenting book? I'm not a neuroscientist or a child-development expert. Instead, I'm drawing on my fifteen-year career as a journalist to help me assess the scientific research and distill it into something readable for tired parents. I've sprinkled in anecdotes from my own life. Not because my experience is vast, and not because it will be exactly like yours, but to give you an idea of the fun, weird, funny, tough moments that make up parenting.

I've focused on baby's first five years because they involve an incredible amount of change. When it comes to mobility, language, empathy, and motor skills, you can't tell the difference between a 30-year-old and a 31-year-old. But the difference between a 1-year-old and a 2-year-old? Remarkable. Amazing. Fascinating. Crazy. More than 90 percent of brain development takes place in those first five years.

So, these early years matter. We're setting baby up for success. And we're establishing our philosophies as parents, which will carry us well beyond five years. The themes in these pages—love, talk, play, connect, discipline, move, slow down—are as important at 2 months old as they are at 2 years old, 5 years old, 15 years old, and even 50 years old. We're all human.

This book is rooted in research. I don't provide a citation within the text for every study, but all of the references are online at www.zerotofive.net. In trying to answer questions, researchers account for all kinds of variables, and they filter out bias as much as possible. It's the best guide we've got.

Still, social-sciences research rarely can give us absolute truth. Here's one example: say researchers are trying to determine whether music lessons make preschoolers smarter. They do a randomized controlled trial, the gold standard. This means they randomly assign half of the kids to take music lessons (the intervention group) and half not (the control group). They administer cognitive tests to both groups of kids before the music lessons and after. How reliable are the results?

Variables include the number of kids the researchers can afford to include in the study, what type of music class they choose, who teaches the class, how many weeks or months the lessons go on, and how frequently or intensely the kids train. Not to mention how many kids drop out of the study along the way, how soon after training the kids are retested, which tests the researchers use, to what extent their analysis attempts to rule out other potential causes for the results (usual suspects include parents' income and IQ), whether previous studies lend credence to the results. And so on and so on.

On top of that, even when the results of a study have been confirmed many times over, they still may not describe your child. If a study concludes that infants need fourteen hours of sleep a day, well, some infants in the study slept eleven hours and some slept nineteen. In the final report, statistics describe the median—and any individual child may fall outside of it.

Not only is every child different, but every parent is, too. All of these are reasons you may follow a piece of advice and get a different result, or not follow a piece of advice and get the same result. You just have to try things and see what works for *your* baby.

Use this book as a guide, both to starting down a good path and to staying on the path you choose. Enjoy the photographs. (Don't worry—none of our homes look this tidy when a photographer's not coming by.) Don't feel the need to follow all seventy tips, either. Once baby arrives, as much as you can, relax.

I know we all have lots of questions. But in the process of writing this book, I found what we've all known all along. What really matters in parenting are the big things: being responsive to baby's needs, truly being present when you're together, talking to baby a ton, being firm but warm in discipline, lots of hugs . . . and sleep.

This book is about how to do those things, which will help you lay the foundation for raising a pretty great kid: smart, happy, social, emotionally healthy, moral, curious, loved.

Best of luck to both of us.

Tracy

www.zerotofive.net

Prepare

Pregnant women tend to have a long to-do list. Put "weekly massages" on the list, and don't fret about the rest. Baby's needs are minimal: a couple key nutrients, whatever sleep and exercise you can manage, and low stress. Spend your time cultivating friendships.

Andréa (32 weeks)

Peace and quiet, please (at first)

Can you turn your embryo into a genius in the womb?

No. For decades, product manufacturers have preyed on vulnerable parents-to-be: give birth to a smarter, calmer, more attentive baby who can already spell!

It started in 1979 with Prenatal University, a twice-daily program in which you pressed your pregnant belly while teaching your fetus words such as "pat," "shake," and "rub." Then came the Pregaphone, which amplified your voice into the womb so that you could communicate even earlier with baby. You placed a plastic funnel on your belly and spoke into a mouthpiece connected via a tube. Today's descendants include a belt that emits heartbeat sounds. You wrap it around your pregnant belly for two hours a day to train your fetus to discriminate sounds. The claim: it will "enrich your unborn child's forming cognitive, empathic, and creative skills."

Lured into the marketing copy, you can't help but wonder, "What if it really does work?" Save your money. No commercial product that claims to boost the braininess of a developing fetus has ever been scientifically proven to do anything useful.

Baby's needs are simple

Perhaps baby is too busy to bother with any interference from products. In the first half of pregnancy, baby starts creating her first brain cells—neurons—at the crazy rapid rate of 250,000 per minute. In the second half of pregnancy, the brain begins connecting those neurons, creating 700 synapses per second in the first few years of life. All baby needs at this stage is the nourishment you provide by eating well, exercising, and reducing your stress.

Bolster your friendships

We tend not to live near our families, and who pops over
for tea anymore when there's txt msgs and Facebook?

We're increasingly isolated. But taking care of a baby is one thing you should not try to do alone. Parents need the emotional and practical support, and babies benefit from exposure to plenty of people. Social isolation can stress you and your marriage, in turn creating an environment harmful to baby.

You're going to need help. And it's up to you to make sure you get it.

You'll need friends to . . .
- bond with while your babies, preferably the same age, play together.
- watch baby while you sleep, shower, get a pedicure, or just do whatever.
- bring you dinner in the early weeks, when you won't want meals to involve much more than finding a fork.
- babysit, so you and your partner can have a regular date night.
- join you for girls' night or guys' night.

Apart from your existing friends, family, and neighbors, where can you find these people?

Plan dates with other parents-to-be from your childbirth education class.

Join a social group for new parents on meetup.com.

Ask around your neighborhood. You might be surprised by the number of resources for new parents. My neighborhood, for example, has a message-board group for parents, a yoga studio with prenatal and mom & baby classes, a café with a baby play area, a children's museum, classes for parents (breastfeeding, babywearing, bitch sessions), classes for babies (music, movement, swimming, story time at the library), new-parent support groups, and parents' nights out hosted by churches, community centers, and baby gyms. Before baby, I didn't know most of these existed.

Talk to strangers. Strike up a conversation with another parent or parent-to-be at the park or grocery store—as simple as "Aww, how old is your baby? What is she doing these days?" or "How are you holding up?" Share something honest. Don't pretend everything's perfect and perpetuate the unrealistic expectations we place on ourselves. Then, don't leave without exchanging contact info: "Hey, let me give you my e-mail address."

TRY THIS

Before baby, invite your dearest friends over for a cooking party, and stock up on freezer-friendly meals. Nourishingmeals.com has ideas for new moms.

As your due date nears, sign up with an online meal registry. This is a huge help in organizing the visitors who, bless them, offer to bring you hot meals.

Eating for two? Not exactly

When you're pregnant, everyone wants you to eat a lot.

"Are you having a craving?" my husband would ask eagerly, ready to make a late-night snack run. "Here, finish these," friends ordered, pushing the fries in my direction. "Go for it," colleagues said as I went for seconds or thirds. "You're eating for two!"

Eventually a couple things sank in:

- You may be eating for two, but one of you is very, very small.
- You need only 300 extra calories a day in the first trimester. And only 350 extra in the second trimester. (That's one eight-grain roll at Starbucks.) And only 450 extra calories in the third. (A couple of oranges with your roll.)

A better way to think of "eating for two"

Focus instead on providing baby with two key nutrients:

Folic acid

What it does: cuts risk of neural tube defects by 76 percent

What it is: vitamin B9

How to get it: leafy greens (spinach, asparagus, turnip greens, lettuce), legumes (beans, peas, lentils), sunflower seeds, prenatal vitamins

When to eat it: four weeks before conception and during the first four weeks of pregnancy

Omega-3s

What they do: aid normal brain development. Babies whose moms got enough omega-3s (300 mg of DHA per day) were better at memory, recognition, attention, and fine motor skills at 6 months old.

What they are: essential fatty acids (ALA, DHA, and EPA), part of the membranes that make up a neuron

How to get them: Eat at least twelve ounces per week of oily fish with low concentrations of mercury. Flaxseed oil isn't converted by the body efficiently enough. Algae-derived DHA capsules (600 mg per day) have potential but are less studied.

When to eat them: Now. Then keep it up.

THE RESEARCH

In a study of twelve thousand women, the less seafood women ate during pregnancy, the greater their risk of having children with verbal IQs in the lowest quartile at 8 years old; behavioral problems at 7 years old; and poor social, communication, and fine motor skills in the early years.

The researchers concluded that any mercury you'd ingest from twelve ounces of fish per week is much less problematic than missing out on the omega-3s from the fish.

"We recorded no evidence to lend support to the warnings of the US advisory that pregnant women should limit their fish consumption," the researchers wrote.

less mercury	more mercury
Salmon	Swordfish
Shrimp	King mackerel
Sardines	Tilefish
Scallops	Shark
Catfish	
Pollock	
Tuna (Wild Planet)	

Exercise thirty minutes a day

If you work out, keep it up. If you don't work out, start.

Doctors used to tell pregnant women to go easy on the exercise. Turns out they were being conservative because so few studies had been done on exercise during pregnancy.

More recent research shows that exercise is so beneficial, it outweighs the miniscule potential risk to baby's health. Signs of risk to the baby don't even begin to show up until you're exercising at a level that feels like an all-out sprint.

THE EFFECT OF EXERCISE ON BABY

Exercise intensity	What happens to baby
Moderate or vigorous (*20 minutes of swimming, walking or running four-plus days a week*)	Baby's heart rate, breathing rate, and umbilical blood flow increase nicely along with yours
Strenuous (*A heart rate at 90% or more of maximum; athletes who are used to pushing their bodies very hard*)	Baby's heart rate and umbilical blood flow dip—but return to normal within 2½ minutes

 **DO IT NOW**   What will you do for exercise? Be specific about the day and time.

Benefits for mom and baby

Exercise benefits the brain, not just the body:

- Exercise increases blood flow, which stimulates the body to make more blood vessels. More blood vessels give the brain more access to oxygen and energy.
- Aerobic exercise also increases BDNF (brain-derived neurotrophic factor), a chemical that grows new neurons. BDNF helps keep existing neurons going by making them less susceptible to damage and stress.
- BDNF karate-chops the toxic effects of stress hormones, including cortisol. In turn, baby's stress-response system and limbic system can develop normally.

Cardio beats weights

Strength training doesn't affect the brain like aerobic exercise does. A combination is great, but if you're pressed for time and energy, go with aerobic exercise. Swimming tops the list. The water supports your weight and disperses excess heat from your belly. The exercise works your entire body. Even if you're just bouncing along in the pool during senior swim, you'll feel so much better. Your impressively swollen ankles will, too.

Listen to your body

How much exercise is too much? Not enough research has been done to know for sure. Maybe that's why everyone says: Listen to your body.

I thought pregnant women weren't supposed to go running or bicycling, so I cut back on exercise when I got pregnant. Soon, I didn't feel healthy. Mid-pregnancy, I went back to my active lifestyle, respecting my mood in terms of how intensely I exercised. I felt so much better. For me, around eight months pregnant was the right time to scale back and just stroll around the neighborhood.

Pregnant women—not used to working out—began exercising four times a week for forty-five to sixty minutes at a time. They started at about 12 weeks pregnant and continued through 36 weeks, doing things like hilly walks and step aerobics. Compared with women who didn't exercise, the exercisers were more fit, fewer had C-sections, and they recovered more quickly after delivery. In another study, women who were 28–32 weeks pregnant ran on a treadmill to exhaustion, and the babies experienced only a brief blip in heart rate and blood flow.

Sing or read to your belly

Newborns can recognize a song or story they heard in the womb.

In a quiet place, pregnant women read a three-minute story excerpted from *The Cat in the Hat* by Dr. Seuss. The women read out loud twice a day for the last six weeks of pregnancy.

After the babies were born, researchers gave them pacifiers attached to machines that could measure their sucking. Stronger sucking triggered audio of their mother reading the story. Weaker sucking triggered audio of her reading an unfamiliar story. The newborns sucked more strongly. They wanted to hear their story! (Or, at least, its familiar rhythms and intonations.)

Your baby, too, likely will find familiar words or songs to be soothing. You can try reciting them as soon as baby arrives.

While you're still pregnant, don't bother reciting anything to baby until your third trimester. Before that, baby can't hear you.

BILLIONS OF BERRIES FOR BLACKBERRY JAMBLE

My husband read *Jamberry*, by Bruce Degen, each night to my belly in the last couple months of my pregnancy. Turns out baby can't really hear dad's voice before birth. (We didn't know!) Mom's voice—resonating through and amplified by her body—is what baby can hear over the din of whooshes, sloshes, gurgles, and heartbeats in the womb. Still, my husband's reading provided a lovely bonding time for us. And the book became a favorite bedtime story for baby.

 DO IT NOW Which song will you sing? Which book will you read?

Stress less

Are you thinking you'll move to a new city, start an intense new job, buy a new house, and finish remodeling just days before your new baby is born?

Here's a better idea: weekly massages, lazy weekend mornings, and dinners spent laughing with friends.

That's because toxic stress during the last few months of pregnancy transfers directly to baby. Excessive stress can

- make baby more irritable and less consolable;
- inhibit baby's motor skills, attention, and ability to concentrate;
- damage baby's stress-response system, causing fight-or-flight hormones to stick around too long; and
- shave an average of eight points off baby's IQ (the difference between average and bright).

How to identify toxic stress

Not all stress is bad, of course. And not all people react to the same stress in the same way. For example, at nine months pregnant, I was racing to finish editing a book. I found the late nights, tight deadlines, and clashing personalities invigorating. Friends thought I was crazy.

The problem is when you feel you have no control over the things stressing you out. Unrelenting stress is the main culprit. Our bodies just aren't built to handle a sustained assault of fight-or-flight stress hormones. An overly demanding job, a chronic illness, poverty, losing a job, an abusive relationship—these are examples of toxic stress.

Pregnancy does create a buffer against stress. Women, pregnant and not, were exposed to the same stressor, and the pregnant women had lower heart rates and cortisol levels. But if you're experiencing chronic stress or anxiety, especially starting in the second trimester, make it a priority to remedy your situation.

If you can't manage to lower your stress during pregnancy, focus on creating a trusting relationship with your newborn baby (see page 38). This has been shown to mitigate the effects of prenatal stress.

THE RESEARCH

Ice storm babies fall behind

When a freezing rain fell on eastern Canada in 1998, more than a million people lost electricity for up to forty days, and a hundred thousand families were shuttled into emergency shelters.

Women who were pregnant during all this were, understandably, stressed in a toxic way. It turns out their children were, too: at age 5½, the kids had lower IQs and poorer language abilities than kids whose mothers weren't affected by the storm.

DO IT NOW

List any areas causing you toxic stress. What big or small steps can you take to regain control?

What will you do for yourself to reduce stress in general?

Share the chores equally

Women in two-income households still do most of the work around the house.

This imbalance is a major minefield that new parents face, especially because baby brings so many new chores. It's also one of the most frequently cited sources of marital conflict. Find a fair solution, and it might save your marriage. (Hey, it might even improve your sex life. A study of nearly seven thousand couples found that as men's share of the weekly housework increases, couples have sex a little more often.)

Bottom line: if you're both working outside the home, household duties need to be shared fairly.

Gay couples are much better at this than straight couples, studies show, because they can't fall back on the assumptions that come with traditional gender roles. They have to start from scratch and divvy up every single task.

This is what you need to do, too.

A ton of work

My husband and I were pretty surprised by the increase in housework that came with having a baby. This may be because, focused on our careers, we had done as little of it as possible. For example, we used to do laundry every two weeks, if we felt like it. Baby's cloth diapers and major spit-up habit meant we suddenly found ourselves doing laundry every two days.

We used to dirty one or two pans for dinner—if we weren't eating out. Plenty of nights we'd cook some pasta, stir in some spinach, and open a jar of sauce. Or toss a pizza in the oven. When baby started eating solid foods, I spent a lot more time cooking fresh produce, beans, and grains. Suddenly we were cleaning a whole pile of kitchen gear every night.

Not to mention wiping off and sweeping up food smeared on the table and dropped on the floor three meals a day. Or picking up toys and the contents of drawers constantly strewn across the house. Or making sure the floors were passably clean, since baby spent so much time on them.

You get the point. Housework goes from "if we get to it" weekly to "must be done" several times daily.

So you can imagine how resentment will quickly build if one person shoulders an unfair amount of that work.

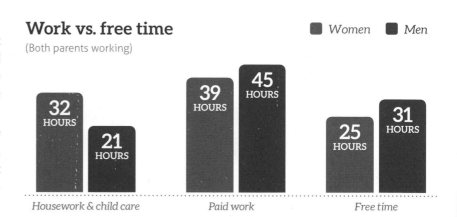

Work vs. free time
(Both parents working)

■ Women ■ Men

Housework & child care	Paid work	Free time
32 HOURS / 21 HOURS	39 HOURS / 45 HOURS	25 HOURS / 31 HOURS

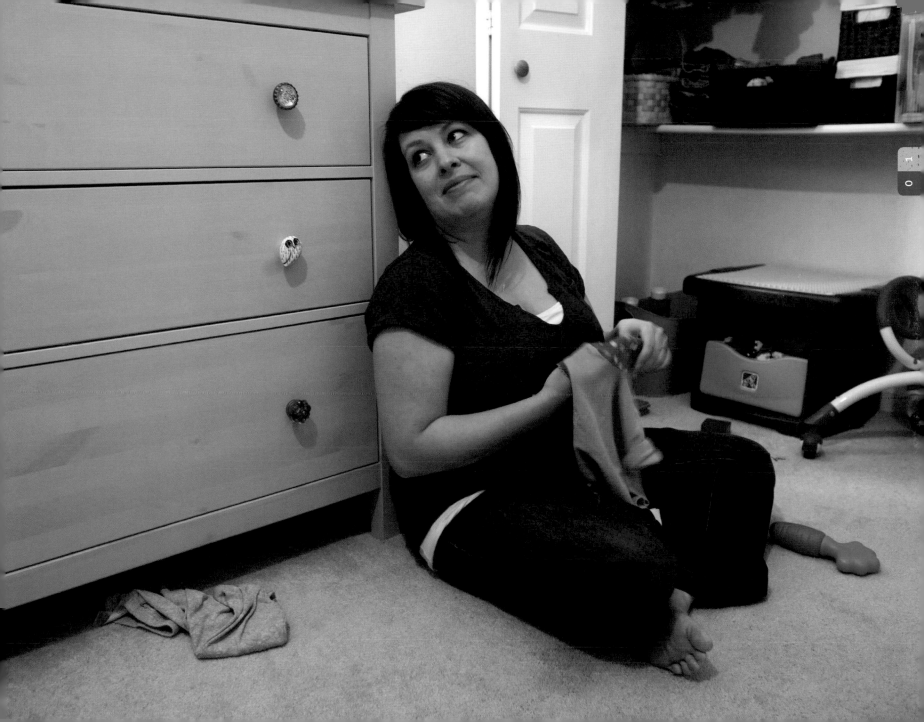

Who will do which chores?

People tend to be satisfied with their contribution to household work—and dissatisfied with their partner's contribution, studies show. And both parties feel underappreciated. So putting things down on paper is a clear, data-driven way to get on the same page.

With your partner, write down the household tasks each of you is responsible for, or use the list at right as inspiration. If the list is lopsided, decide how to balance it. One strategy is to claim chores you're each good at or don't mind doing. Compromise on the rest: flip a coin, trade off, or do them together.

Doing some chores together (say, one person cooks the main dish and the other makes the sides, or both of you clean at the same time) is good for your relationship, too.

FIRST SHIFT, SECOND SHIFT, THIRD SHIFT

The house turns into such a wreck each day, my husband and I made a pact. He would clean the house in the morning, after feeding baby breakfast and playing, so I wasn't starting the day with a mess. I would clean the house before he returned from work, so he wasn't coming home to chaos. Then we would tidy up together after dinner. When we stick to our plan, we find that our moods improve, and so do our attitudes toward each other.

Chore	Mine	Yours
Dishes	○	○
Meals		
Grocery shopping	○	○
Breakfast	○	○
Lunch	○	○
Dinner	○	○
Laundry		
Washing & drying	○	○
Folding & putting away	○	○
Garbage, recycling, compost	○	○
Bathrooms	○	○
Vacuuming	○	○
Dusting	○	○
Repairs	○	○
Paying bills	○	○
Scheduling the calendar	○	○

Chore	Mine	Yours
Getting baby ready to leave	○	○
Packing/unpacking diaper bag	○	○
Putting baby to bed		
Naps	○	○
Nighttime	○	○
Caring for baby		
(feeding, changing diapers, playing)		
Weekdays		
Morning	○	○
Afternoon	○	○
Evening	○	○
Nighttime wakings	○	○
Weekends		
Morning	○	○
Afternoon	○	○
Evening	○	○
Nighttime wakings	○	○

TRY THIS

One quick way to make sure you're left doing most of the work is to continually criticize your partner's help. Cut each other some slack. Just say, "Thanks. I really appreciate that you put the dishes in the dishwasher."

Percy, father of Amelia (4) & Honorio (5 weeks)

If you're suffering, get help

Depression among new parents is more common than you might think, and not discussed as much as it should be.

Postpartum depression can hit both parents. And if mom is depressed, it's more likely that dad will be, too. The exact cause of postpartum depression isn't known, but hormones, lack of sleep, and stress are thought to be contributing factors. Fortunately, postpartum depression is treatable. Sooner is better.

Depression affects baby's brain, too. Depressed parents are less responsive to their babies, and they engage less positively with their babies. At 9 months old, the babies are

- less social,
- not as good at regulating their behavior,
- more emotionally negative,
- more easily stressed.

Ways to prepare
Find a counselor before baby comes, so you'll have a number to call if you need it. Ask your doctor, midwife, doula, or friends for a recommendation. You want someone who can see you immediately, not in six weeks.

Designate a close friend or family member, or both, to tell you if he or she sees symptoms of depression in you, because you might not see them in yourself.

When to get help
A couple weeks of "baby blues"—fatigue, sadness, and worry—are normal. But if you feel anxious and overwhelmed most of the time, for longer than two weeks, get help. No excuses. No judgment. For men, common symptoms include feeling tired and irritable, escaping (into work, sports, alcohol), or acting more controlling, aggressive, or reckless. For women, see the next page.

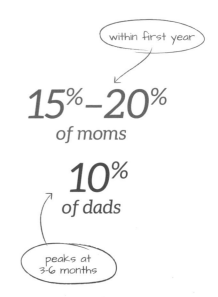

Both parents are vulnerable to depression

within first year

15%–20%
of moms

10%
of dads

peaks at 3-6 months

THINK ABOUT IT

Do I have postpartum depression?

If you have had a baby within the last twelve months, and you have experienced some of these symptoms for more than two weeks, please find help. This list comes from Katherine Stone, publisher of PostpartumProgress.com, the most widely read blog on postpartum depression.

- You feel overwhelmed. Not like "Hey, this new-mom thing is hard." More like "I can't do this and I'm never going to be able to do this."

- You feel guilty because you believe you should be handling new motherhood better than this. You feel like your baby deserves better.

- You don't feel bonded to your baby. You're not having that mythical mommy bliss that you see on TV or read about in magazines.

- You continually feel irritated or angry. You have no patience. Everything annoys you. You feel resentment toward your baby, or your partner, or your friends who don't have babies. You feel out-of-control rage.

- You feel nothing but emptiness and numbness. You are just going through the motions.

- You feel sadness to the depths of your soul. You can't stop crying, even when there's no real reason to be crying.

- You can't bring yourself to eat, or perhaps the only thing that makes you feel better is eating.

- You can't sleep, no matter how tired you are. Or maybe all you can do is sleep. Whichever it is, your sleeping is completely screwed up, and it's not just because you have a newborn.

- You can't concentrate. You can't focus. You can't think of the words you want to say. You can't remember what you were supposed to do. You can't make a decision. You feel like you're in a fog.

- You feel disconnected. You feel strangely apart from everyone, like there's an invisible wall between you and the rest of the world.

- You might be having thoughts of running away and leaving your family behind.

- You've thought of driving off the road, or taking too many pills, or finding some other way to end this misery.

- You know something is wrong, that the way you are feeling is NOT right. You wonder if you've "gone crazy."

- You are afraid that this is your new reality and that you've lost the "old you" forever.

- You are afraid that if you reach out for help, people will judge you. Or that your baby will be taken away.

Used with permission

Expect conflict as a couple

Two-thirds of couples struggle with their marriages soon after baby arrives.

The majority of couples report a drop in marital satisfaction after baby. It hits its lowest point when the kids are teenagers, and it doesn't rebound until the kids move out.

Why is this important for baby? Because if you're stressed out and fighting—or headed toward divorce—you're creating a home environment that hurts your child's brain development.

A few factors put you at higher risk for a drop in marital satisfaction:

- If the mother's parents are divorced or had high levels of conflict
- If you lived together before getting married
- If you had a baby soon after getting married (waiting gives you more time to get on the same page about relationship responsibilities)

- If you have a lot of negative communication and didn't handle conflict well before baby
- If one of you didn't want a baby but caved in

Well, that covers just about all of us.

The good news

In a third of relationships, marital satisfaction stays the same or improves after baby. What are they doing right? They're choosing empathy (see page 127), dealing with conflicts lovingly (see page 128), sharing the chores (see page 16), and building a great support network (see page 8).

You can make a concerted effort to do these things, too.

The transition to parenthood is tough

Four studies of marital satisfaction ask different questions but arrive at similar answers.
Source: C. Walker, "Some Variations in Marital Satisfaction." Copyright Elsevier. Used with permission.

■ *Study 1*   ■ *Study 2*   ■ *Study 3*   ■ *Study 4*

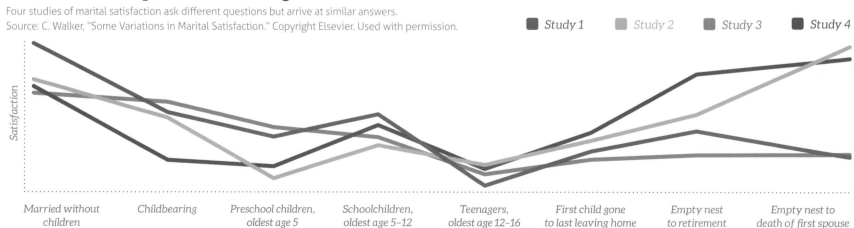

Satisfaction

| Married without children | Childbearing | Preschool children, oldest age 5 | Schoolchildren, oldest age 5–12 | Teenagers, oldest age 12–16 | First child gone to last leaving home | Empty nest to retirement | Empty nest to death of first spouse |

Know you can't truly be prepared

You're going to be clueless, and that's OK.

Having a baby is a culture shock. As much time as you spent planning for this, it all becomes real quite suddenly. You don't speak baby's language; you're not sure what she's trying to tell you. You feel incompetent when it comes to the most basic things, like how much this little human needs to eat or how she wants to sleep. You've never been in such close contact with spit-up, drool, pee, and poop—things you'd previously tried to avoid. You barely recognize your house, as cleaning falls to the wayside and baby stuff piles up. Your senses become heightened: you start to hear baby's cries when there are none, or you bolt upright in bed with the urge to make sure baby's still alive. Time ceases to have meaning. When baby cries inconsolably, minutes feel like hours. When you look into baby's eyes, cuddle, and kiss baby's soft skin, hours feel like minutes.

It's an adventure, and generally you feel up for it. Plus, baby sleeps a ton at first, giving you a little time to adjust.

However, many first-time parents also face an additional challenge that hits hard. It could be postpartum depression. It could be that baby is colicky, or underweight, or not latching at the breast, or premature. It could be that you're an ambitious person and haven't yet figured out that you're trying to do too much. For my husband and me, it was sleep deprivation.

Feeding baby was taking two hours—and you're supposed to feed a newborn at least every three hours. I wasn't producing much milk, but I didn't want to give up on breastfeeding. So the hospital had us taping a tiny tube to my breast, and passing milk through it using a syringe. That way, baby was still "nursing." Getting this tube to stay in place *and* getting baby to latch was indescribably time-consuming and frustrating. If baby let go, we'd have to start all over. Then switch breasts. Then I'd use a breast pump. Then my husband would sterilize all the equipment. We were reeling from lack of sleep.

My husband and I rarely fight, but suddenly we were arguing over critical things like whether the phrase "Don't cry over spilled milk" referred to the child or the mother. Emotions ran high or low, nothing in between. I remember walking down the street in broad daylight and bursting into tears. My husband blurted out, "Where are the *joys* of parenthood?" Within ten days, we ditched the syringe, switched to bottles, I pumped less often, and we caught up on sleep.

Gradually, we defined, then accepted, then embraced, our new normal as parents. Soon enough, we felt like we were getting the hang of things. And you will, too.

Not that parenting will suddenly become easy. With a baby, just about every day has highs and lows. Woven throughout moments of frustration, anxiety, and exhaustion are moments of such immense joy, strength, determination, humor, and love. These blissful times more than erase the hard ones.

I remember one sunny day when my baby was 7 or 8 months old. Walking through a beautiful forested park, I told her how the leaves had fallen from the trees. I sat in a swing with her facing me in my lap, and as we swung, she leaned against my chest and smiled a supremely content little smile. This made such happiness well up inside me that I laughed out loud, hugged her to me, and said, "I love you so much!"

Moments like these come from a deep connection with a person. You can feel it with friends or lovers occasionally, but with a child you get to feel it several times a day in such a pure sense. It makes you realize that's what's most important in life—our connections as humans.

Maybe this is why veteran parents forget to tell us first-timers how hard parenting can be. If so, it's a pretty good reason.

Envision baby all grown up

Take a moment to imagine your child as an adult.

What kind of work do you hope she is doing? What values do you hope he has? What life skills? What kind of relationship does your baby have with you, family, friends, and partners?

At first it might be difficult to imagine your baby being anything but a baby. It was for my husband and me. We did this exercise with Seattle-based parent coach Nita Talwar. Busy just keeping our heads above water, we spent more time worrying about baby's next nap than pondering what our child would be like twenty years from now. Quickly, though, I could see the power of looking ahead.

"It's easier to get where you want to go," Nita pointed out, "if you have a map."

Stating the skills and character traits that you value helps you prioritize how you want to parent. My husband and I each put "good communicator; articulate" on our lists—not surprising, given that we're both writers and editors. I'm naturally a listener rather than a talker, but I overrode my quiet tendencies to talk to our baby a lot (see page 48). If we hadn't stopped to think about what we value, I might have let that slide.

Which brings up another point: you might have to grow, too

Do you hope your daughter has a loving, healthy relationship with her partner? Then you'll need to show her that kind of relationship. Do you hope she has empathy and respect for others? Then you'll need to model that.

Do you hope your son values helping others? Then you'll need to help others. Do you hope he knows how to solve problems in a calm way without being hurtful? Then you'll have to do so.

What image do you want your baby to have of what a good father or mother is? Then . . . you get the idea.

This might require making some changes in your life.

No one wants to hear that, right? Some days I think: I'm just doing the best I can, based on who I am. Other days, I'm surprised by my desire to become a better person for my baby.

 **DO IT NOW** Write down the values and life skills you hope your child exhibits as an adult, twenty or thirty years from now. How will you need to change in order to model those things?

TRY THIS

During any given wonderful or terrible moment, you think, "I'll remember this forever." You won't. That would require remembering nearly every single day of baby's life. If you're like me, you can barely remember what happened yesterday.

So, since pregnancy, I've kept a "One Line a Day" journal. One line per day is just about the right level of commitment. OK, one line every few days. Mine is a five-year journal: each page is devoted to one date, with space to write about each of the five years.

It's neat to be reminded of what was happening on a certain date in previous years—and to wonder what my baby will glean from the journal when she's all grown up.

Sarah (36 weeks)

Love

The most important thing you can do with your newborn is to be sensitive to baby's needs. Respond when baby tries to engage with you. Match those smiles, coos, and gazes. Comfort those cries. Cuddle up, skin to skin. Fall in love.

Madeline & Claire (5 weeks)

Prepare to be amazed

Babies' minds are working, working, testing hypotheses, and making use of an incredible set of innate cognitive abilities.

A newborn less than one hour old can imitate. Even though he's never seen a face before, including his own, a baby is born knowing how to stick out his tongue at you, if you stick out yours.

Babies shun the bad guy. Babies 6 and 10 months old watched a show in which one toy helps another toy up a hill. A third toy pushes it back down the hill. The researchers then brought in the helper toy and the hinderer toy for the babies to play with. Babies were much more likely to reach for the helper toy.

Babies can predict an action. When 9-month-olds reach for an object, their brain's motor region is activated. And when 9-month-olds simply watch an adult reach for an object, that same motor region is activated. Watching the adult a second time, the babies' motor region activates just prior to the adult reaching—in effect predicting the adult's action.

Babies can make predictions based on probability. Infants 10 to 12 months old were tested to see whether they preferred a pink lollipop or a black one. Next, babies were shown two jars: one with more pink lollipops and one with more black. Researchers then plucked a lollipop from each jar (shielded now, so baby couldn't tell which color lollipop was chosen) and covered each lollipop with a cup. About 80 percent of the time, the infants chose the cup most likely to contain their favorite color of lollipop.

Do something one time, and a 14-month-old can repeat it a week later in the same context. Researchers created a box that would light up when touched. As babies watched, experimenters leaned forward from the waist and touched their foreheads to the box. Brought back to the lab a week later, two-thirds of babies remembered. They leaned forward and touched their own foreheads to the box. The researchers tried longer delays, too—and some babies remembered *four months later.*

Babies will give you broccoli. An 18-month-old understands that your wants might differ from hers. In front of the child, an experimenter ate raw broccoli, making a happy face ("Mmm!"), and then goldfish crackers, making a disgusted face ("Yuck!"). Then the experimenter held out her hand to the child and said, "Could you give me some?" Even though they prefer crackers, 18-month-olds gave her raw broccoli—what the experimenter said she liked. The experiment also was done with 15-month-olds. Babies at that age always hand over crackers, which is what they like.

Babies are taking statistics. Babies take in everything from the environment around them—sounds, visual scenes, language—and calculate the frequency with which something occurs. In the case of language, babies use these statistics to determine which letter sounds to continue discriminating between and which to drop.

Babies are designed to learn. Babies absorb information from many sources at once, lighting up a host of neurotransmitters—many more than adult brains have—that leap into action for rapid learning. Then, like scientists, babies and young children create hypotheses and run experiments about the world and about human nature. Researcher Alison Gopnik calls young children "the research and development division of the human species."

SEE WHAT BABY CAN DO

I'm continually impressed by the things my baby can do, say, remember, and repeat. Before babies can talk, you tend to assume they don't understand anything you're saying. They do. Dressing my baby in a shirt at 10 months old, I asked her to put her arm in the sleeve—and she did. When baby started talking, it was too late to take back some of the things my husband and I had said to her. "Butt balm for the butt!" she'd repeat during diaper changes.

If I give baby enough time, patiently waiting instead of jumping in to help, she's often able to twist on a lid, snap a buckle, find a towel and wipe up a spill, or put away an item before moving on to the next thing. At 20 months old, I was surprised to learn she could finish the sentences of favorite books, if I paused. Reading *Corduroy*, about a small bear in green overalls who's missing a button, I'd start, "I didn't know I'd . . ." and she'd finish, "lost a button, said to self. I'll go FIND it!"

It's easy to underestimate a baby. Keep testing your baby's boundaries—and prepare to be amazed.

Ross, Jess & Naomi (14 months)

Create a feeling of safety

Yes, you should anchor your furniture to the walls and lock away your cleaning supplies. But that's not the kind of safety I'm talking about here.

Your baby's strongest need is to feel safe with you.

Children are exquisitely sensitive to their environments. If you create an environment of safety, love, and emotional stability, good things happen:

- Baby's brain develops a healthy stress-response system, efficiently deploying and then reducing stress hormones as needed.
- With stress hormones in balance, baby's neural circuits for learning and reasoning are protected. The cardiovascular and immune systems can function properly.
- Life's smaller stresses ("No shirt! I don't *want* it!") become chances for growth, because supportive relationships buffer the negative effects of stress.
- Baby sees your healthy responses to stressful experiences and gets practice responding in healthy ways.

In a home with high levels of conflict, on the other hand, baby's stress-response system is damaged. The system is either forced into a state of constant high alert or dulled into reacting too mildly to stress. Baby is unable to form a trusting attachment with caregivers (see page 38). Later, the child is more likely to be aggressive and delinquent. You might think babies are too young to understand that their parents are fighting. But babies younger than 6 months old can tell something is wrong. Babies' blood pressure and heart rate rise, and so do their levels of the stress hormone cortisol.

How you fight matters

That doesn't mean you can never fight. Not all parents' fights hurt a child's brain development. If, when you argue, you are supportive of your partner and show small signs of affection (see page 128), children learn that you can and will manage conflict in a way that preserves family harmony. If you are hostile with your partner, making threats and lobbing insults, or you're physically aggressive, that's when the conflicts harm kids.

Baby's stress-response system develops over the first year

The kinds of things that stress baby (that is, increase her cortisol level) change as experiences fine-tune baby's stress-response system.

Newborn	Cortisol increases even if baby is picked up
3 months	Being picked up is no longer stressful, but a doctor exam is
6 months	Cortisol is less reactive during a doctor exam and shots
9 months	Being left with a trusted babysitter barely increases cortisol
13 months	Baby can be upset with no increase in cortisol

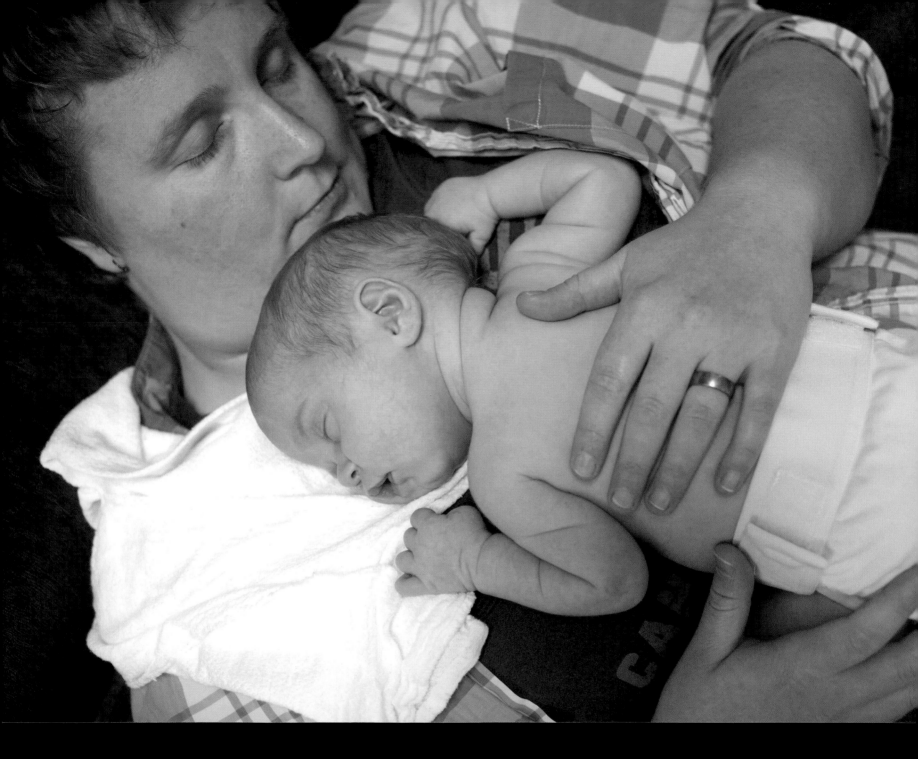

Comfort newborn with the familiar

Thrust into a foreign place, who wouldn't be comforted by the vestiges of home?

Newborns cry because they're hungry or gassy or sleepy or hot or cold or wet. And they cry after you've checked all those things, for reasons that will remain a mystery. Baby's dealing with a lot right now. You can't always solve the problem to stop the crying, but you can comfort baby as he cries.

Scent
Researchers recorded the crying of newborns, a mere 30 minutes old, who were separated from their mothers for an hour. If the babies were exposed to the smell of the mother's amniotic fluid—the protective sac of water baby had been floating in before birth—they cried less than thirty seconds. If not, they cried more than two minutes.

What else is a familiar scent to a newborn? Well, mom, for one. Baby can smell you starting at seven months in the womb—your body odor, even the lotion you rub on your belly each evening. (Might I recommend Almond Supple Skin Oil from L'Occitane? Mmm. Drop hints for your baby shower.) Soon after birth, dad's scent can become familiar, too.

During the painful heel prick to draw baby's blood, babies cried and grimaced much less if they smelled a familiar scent. Mama's milk worked for breastfed babies. The scent of vanilla, which researchers previously had wafted under baby's nose, worked as well.

Sound
If you sang or read to baby during your third trimester of pregnancy (see page 14), use that song or story to comfort baby right after birth.

Motion
Wrap baby to your body and walk (see page 180)—a very familiar cadence to baby.

Sniff, sniff? Newborns cry less
Median crying time during separation from mom, when exposed to her amniotic fluid vs. no exposure.

Exposed — **29** SECONDS

Not exposed — **135** SECONDS

GOOD TO KNOW

Baby's first three months are called "the fourth trimester." The evolutionary theory is that babies could use more time in the womb—but they must be born early so their heads fit through the birth canal.

To ease baby's transition outside the womb, parents try to replicate the noisy, cozy, warm, rock-and-roll conditions inside the womb. That's why Harvey Karp's "Five S's" work so well to comfort baby: swaddling, side or stomach position, swinging, shushing, and sucking. See happiestbaby.com for details.

Cuddle with baby

Babies are happy with almost constant contact in their first few months. Touch feels good!

Affectionate touch is essential for cognitive and emotional development. More technically: touch triggers the release of certain neurotransmitters, which soothe the nervous system and lower baby's levels of cortisol, a stress hormone. Touch signals safety to the brain.

At the extreme negative end, babies not touched for days on end simply stare off into space. Their stress-response system is damaged, creating a cascade of negative effects.

Ways to get close

In baby's first weeks, you're in a haze just trying to get the hang of all this feeding, burping, napping, pooping, and generally keeping baby alive. Then, at some point in the day, all of those things have occurred, and you may wonder: Now what do we do?

Instead of setting baby in a swing to stare at mobiles, cuddle up:

Go skin to skin. Let your newborn, wearing only a diaper, rest on mom's or dad's bare chest. Snuggle with baby in bed the same way. Breastfeed topless at home. Your skin warms baby, but you can also put a blanket over the two of you. Being skin to skin, or nursing, when the doctor gives baby heel pricks or shots also lowers baby's stress.

Wrap baby against your body. Use a soft-structured carrier, sling, or wrap while you run your errands, do some chores, or go for a walk. (After you've recovered from the labor, I mean—don't go anywhere at first, if you can help it!) Save the stroller for when baby gets heavy or you need to haul stuff.

Massage baby each day. Researchers found that 4-month-olds who got a daily eight-minute massage were

- in a better mood,
- less anxious and stressed,
- more attentive, and
- sleeping more regularly.

Seems to me like massage does the same for moms . . .

Start with baby on his back, then his tummy. The pressure needs to be moderate, not too light. In India, where baby massage is a centuries-old tradition, women lay baby on their outstretched legs and work vigorously with warm oil. (Search online for a video to get an idea of the amount of pressure.) Talk to, sing to, or smile at baby while you massage. A silent, distant massage only raises baby's stress level. If baby seems agitated, adjust your touch, or try another time—baby may just need a break right now (see page 38).

THE RESEARCH

In one study, preterm babies got skin-to-skin contact ("kangaroo care") each day. Each time researchers followed up, between 6 months old and 10 years old, these babies had more efficient stress responses, more organized sleep patterns, and better executive function than preterm babies cared for in an incubator. The new moms were less anxious, too.

Honorio (5 weeks) & Maribel

Ross & Naomi (14 months)

Tracy & Geneva (23 months)

Nora (2) & Tony

Stacy & Mak (13 months)

Get in sync

Baby loves it when you mimic her facial expressions, coo at her little sounds, and gaze into her eyes.

When baby tries to engage with you in one of those ways, she needs you to respond in kind. This "serve and return" interaction is foundational in wiring baby's brain. It helps the brain develop in a way that supports stress regulation, empathy, and emotional stability. But sometimes baby needs a break.

I was leaning over my newborn on a play mat, laughing and cooing, when baby suddenly turned her head to the left, lost in a million-mile stare. I had an urge to say, "Hello? Where'd you go?"

Then I remembered that when a baby is overstimulated, she tells you by

- turning her head away,
- closing her eyes,
- avoiding your gaze,
- tensing up, or
- suddenly becoming fussy.

It was neat for me to understand what was happening. And it helped me resist my initial urge to bring baby back by calling her name or waving in front of her face. My baby turned back to me just a few moments later, ready to carry on.

Synchrony creates a trusting relationship

Matching baby's lulls by patiently waiting, and then engaging when she does, is a hallmark of responsive, sensitive parenting. You're attuned to baby, aware of baby's cues, and quick to respond to baby's cues. Sensitive parenting helps baby form a trusting relationship with you, called "secure attachment." Parents who continually ignore or reject their baby's bids for interaction and reassurance don't create a trusting relationship. Attachment has nothing to do with whether baby is constantly attached to your body.

EXAMPLES OF ATTACHMENT	
Secure attachment	**Insecure attachment**
Child turns to you for protection and comfort	Child turns away from you when distressed
Child uses you as a base from which to explore the world	Child alternates between clinging and pushing you away

Being out of sync stresses baby

When mama and baby are in sync, their biological rhythms are, too. For example, during face-to-face interaction, their heartbeats become coordinated with a lag of less than one second.

When parent and baby are out of sync, baby gets stressed. Harvard researcher Ed Tronick conducted "still face" experiments in which mothers simply gave a blank stare when their babies wanted to engage. The babies tried smiling, pointing, waving, and screeching, all to no avail. Babies then began to turn away, cry, and slump. When the mothers quit their act, it took their babies a moment to trust them again and reengage. But they did reengage. Building (or breaking) a trusting relationship with baby is a process that happens over several years.

Smile, hug, encourage

A smile, a wink, a hug, or a word of encouragement helps create a positive home environment. When children get attention in positive ways, they are less likely to seek attention in negative ways.

Jerry, Miles (15 months) & Karen

Sonia & Quentin (2)

Arden (3) & Andréa

Include baby

Quality time with baby can mean taking out the garbage together.

Including baby in life's little tasks requires accepting that any task will take much, much longer. But that's OK. Engaging baby in whatever you're doing gives you lots to show baby and lots to talk about, along with little moments you'll cherish.

For part of the day, baby and I have friends to meet, books to read, music to dance to, and walks to go on. But when I need to get stuff done, here are some of the things that work for me:

Showering

- Before baby can sit up: Cradle baby in a portable chair, or surround baby with pillows on the floor within your view.
- Once baby can sit up: Let baby splash, too, on the bathtub floor or in a bucket-style baby bath. I'm very grateful for our Tummy Tub.

Cooking

- Before baby can sit up, put baby in a carrier.
- Prep food at the dining-room table while baby sits in the high chair, or bring the high chair to the kitchen. Talk about all of the ingredients, and pass baby produce to feel or taste.
- Sit baby on the floor with some blocks, pans and utensils, or food samples. Explain the things you're doing.
- Get a stool or "learning tower" so your child can see. Have her help, by throwing away packaging, pouring ingredients into the pot, or stirring.
- I often make a green smoothie in the blender. Baby likes to nibble the pear, twist the lemon halves on the citrus juicer, strip the stems from the kale, and watch everything whirl. As I turn on the blender, I say, "Loud noise in one, two, three—" and we do a little dance.

Laundry

- Let baby put a couple items in the machine, twist some knobs, and watch the spinning clothes—it's TV for babies!
- Play peekaboo while folding laundry.
- Ask your toddler to put away items that belong in his room.
- Make the bed with baby in it. Whip the sheet into the air and let it float down over the two of you.

Cleaning

- Hand over part of the job. Around 18 months, my baby liked to get out the dustpan when I was sweeping, and she'd grab the rag to wipe up spills.
- Enlist baby's help to empty the dishwasher: "Here, put your dish on your shelf. Can you get your stool, and put your spoon in the drawer?"

Fixing stuff

- Your toddler would probably love to help you assemble her new balance bike, remove the old knobs from the dresser drawers, or sit in your suitcase and twist the screwdriver to tighten the handle. Explain as you go.

Errands

- Walk, if you can, or take the bus. People you pass by love to talk with baby, and you see all sorts of interesting things.
- Choose one errand and make a day of it. For example, I once walked to a store five miles away. Baby and I had plenty to look at along the way, we ran into a friend, we stopped for lunch, and we took the bus home. The errand took hours, technically, but it made for a nice day.

Talk

Describe the world to baby in all its richness. "Mmm, pomegranate seeds. Aren't they a beautiful color? A deep red, like rubies." Count the stairs as you walk them. Recount your day. Say anything and everything—just talk a ton. Read every day.

Stacy & Mak (13 months)

Speak in a singsongy voice

The best way to talk with baby is to snuggle in close and use a high, lilting voice with drawn-out vowels.

It's called "parentese." In the first eighteen months, it helps baby pick out and imitate parts of language.

That's because each vowel and word becomes more distinct, so they're easier for baby to discern. The higher pitch matches the limited range of a baby's smaller vocal tract—one-quarter the size of yours.

It's not what you say, it's how you say it

Infants prefer the pitch of parentese to adult speech, according to decades of research:

- Babies' heart rates increased when they heard parentese, even in a foreign language.
- At 5 months old, babies smiled more at approvals and looked worried at disapprovals in parentese.
- At 12 months old, babies asked to look at a picture did so more often when asked in parentese.

TRY THIS

Read a magazine story to your baby, using the same tone and speed you would with your partner. See how your baby reacts. (Mine tries to pinch my lips closed.) Now read it again in parentese. It's pretty funny to look baby in the eyes and say, wide-eyed and smiling, something like, "Unfortunately, encounters with cops are always at the worst moments in your life." But watch baby engage!

Sarah & Opal (3 weeks)

Talk to your baby a ton

If your baby hears a ton of talk in her first three years, she'll have a bigger vocabulary, a higher IQ, and better grades than children who aren't talked to much.

When should you start? In the last ten weeks of pregnancy. Babies begin to absorb language, as the mother's voice reverberates through her body, earlier than researchers realized.

Talk richly

Simplify a description or explanation, but there's no need to avoid using the proper words. Most words are unusual to a baby, right? Instead of just "Look— airplane!" you might say, "That's a *seaplane*. Do you see how the plane has two feet? Those feet are called pontoons. Pontoons let the plane float on the water. A seaplane floats on the water." (To such explanations, my baby replies amenably, "OK, yeah.")

Talk positively

Encourage your child. "Wow, you're learning to pour! Oops, the water spilled. Yeah, it's tricky to line up the cups. We'll clean that up. OK, let's try again—hold your hand here . . ." That's more encouraging than saying, "Let Daddy pour that. You're going to spill it."

Repeat or rephrase baby's words.
"Ball! Yes, you're playing with a ball."

Give positive feedback.
Use more "Good" and "Right" than "Don't," "Stop," and "Bad."

Give polite guidance rather than directives.
"Can you . . . ?" and "Do you . . . ?" and "Oh, thank you!"

Talk directly to baby

Speech that baby simply overhears doesn't provide the same boost in baby's vocabulary or language proficiency. Neither does playing audio or video of someone talking. The brain is electrified by face-to-face interaction, so much so that the presence or absence of that social connection acts as a gate to learning language.

Talk regularly

Children who are talked to more often get a brain boost. It helps to have places to go and people to see, which gives you a world of things to describe and explain. (See page 42 for more ideas.)

Greg & Claire (5 weeks)

Say anything and everything

Newborn and infant

It may feel a little strange to talk this much to someone who doesn't talk back. But you get used to it.

Read out loud. A newspaper story, for example, gives you a chance to catch up on the world (if you can keep baby from ripping the paper and eating it).

Explain what's about to happen to baby. Babies understand more than you think they do, and it helps to give them a little notice before moving them this way and that. "Let's change your diaper. Here comes a wet wipe. Legs up . . . legs down." "I'm going to put on your hat, and then we'll walk outside." "Grandma is going to visit you today."

Narrate your day—whatever you're doing, seeing, thinking, and feeling. Take moments to engage your baby with eye contact, a smile, or a tickle. It doesn't really matter what you talk about.

Examples
Folding laundry: "Oh good, two matching socks. *Two matching socks!* I'm folding the tops together so one doesn't get lost. There we go." "Ooh, a nice warm sheet." (Cover baby's head, then lift it away.) "Where's baby? There's baby!"

Going for a walk: Talk about where you're going today and what you see as you pass by.

Dressing baby: "Let's see, which shirt will you wear today? I'm partial to this one. Over the head!" (Baby flips over and wiggles away.) "Come here, little fishy. We're not done yet!" (Scoot baby back to you with kisses.) "Left arm through. Right arm through. Good. Well, aren't you cute. Aren't you cute!"

Making a bottle: "Fill . . . scoop . . . pour . . . twist . . . shake-shake-shake."

Toddler

Once baby is more active, all this talking gets easier and, I found, feels less silly—even if it doesn't sound less silly.

Examples
Simply describe all the impressive stuff baby is doing. "You opened the drawer. You closed the drawer. Open. Close. Open. Close. Good job! You're pulling the drawer open. You're pushing the drawer closed. Pull. Push. Pull. Push. Ooh, a pen. You found a pen in the drawer. Wow, you took the lid off the pen! I'll take that . . ."

Explain whatever baby seems interested in. "Yes, that's Daddy's helmet. HEL-met. He's putting it on his head. He's buckling the strap under his chin. Now he can safely ride his bike."

Build nouns into sentences. "Lid. This is a lid. A lid goes on top of a pan. I put the lid on top of the pan. Can you put the lid on top of the pan?"

Once baby starts talking, interacting this way becomes even more fun—and impossibly cute. Before you know it, baby starts repeating everything you say. Then you can teach baby to say things you want to hear. Our baby says, "Daddy runs fast!" and "Go, Pack, go!"

(**DO IT NOW**) Which situations will you narrate to baby?

2,100 words per hour?!

Betty Hart tried everything she could think of to improve the vocabularies of the 4-year-olds in the low-income preschool where she was teaching. She couldn't do it. Finally, she and Todd Risley, her graduate supervisor at the University of Kansas, figured out that, by age 4, it was too late.

They wanted to know why.

So they followed forty-two families and recorded every word they said—for one hour per month, over two-and-a-half years.

It took six years to transcribe the resulting thirteen hundred hours of tapes. Hart and Risley then analyzed the differences in the way rich and poor parents speak with their children. They studied the quality of the talking from many angles: Did the mix of nouns and verbs matter? The vocabulary level? Whether the talk was positive or negative?

The number of words turned out to be the most interesting variable:

- A child in a family on welfare heard an average of 600 words an hour, while a child in a professional family heard 2,100 words an hour.
- By age 4, children of professional parents had heard forty-eight million words addressed to them; children in poor families had heard thirteen million. No wonder poor kids were behind in vocabulary and speech acquisition—differences that affected their later educational abilities.
- Children's language skills at age 3 predicted their language skills at age 9 or 10.

How much is the "ton of talk" baby needs to hear to have a bigger vocabulary, a higher IQ, and better grades? Researchers found that it's 21,000 words a day, or 2,100 words an hour. Sound daunting? I thought so at first.

As it turns out, 2,100 words an hour does not mean a stream of constant chatter. It's about fifteen minutes' worth of talking over an hour.

Parents also tend to speak in chunks averaging only four words: "Hi, beautiful baby." "Who's that in the mirror? Is that you?" "Oops, Mommy forgot her keys." "Where are your shoes?" Simple phrases—they count. These parents weren't riffing on the theory of relativity.

In the study, professional families averaged 487 of these utterances per hour. Low-income families averaged 176 per hour.

Vocab explosion!

Age	Average child can understand
1½ years	100 words
3 years	1,000 words
6 years	6,000 words (only 44,000 more to go . . .)

A LITTLE TEST AT THE SINK: 60 WORDS TAKES 26 SECONDS

OK, let's wash your hands. This is the cold water. No, that's the hot water. We'll put a little soapy on your palm. Yep, rub, rub, rub. You're rubbing your hands together. Ooh, I see lots of bubbles. Let's get the backs of your hands. Good. OK, time to rinse! Rub, rub, rub under the water. All right, let's dry.

Read together

Look at the words on the page and say them out loud.
That's how one reads a book to a child, I assumed. Nope.

Babies & babblers

Before 6 months

Think of "reading" more as exploring the concept of books. Read sturdy board books, and let baby chew corners. Or read aloud whatever magazine or novel you're into at the moment (or were into, before baby). This way, you'll be exposing baby to the sounds of language and getting a break from "all things baby."

6–12 months

Talk about the pictures. Encourage baby to point: "Where's the yellow flower?" Let baby turn pages and feel textures. Baby doesn't care much about the plot at this point. Don't feel like you have to finish the book.

12–18 months

Engage baby with dramatic readings, different voices, big expressions, and gestures. When a bee goes "buzz!" you can make the sound and come in close to land a kiss. When a character goes fast or slow, you can use your fingertips to crawl or run up baby's belly.

Read together every day, even if just for five or ten minutes.

Talkers

1½ years–3 years

Help your child become the storyteller. Each time you read the same book, do less reading yourself, and let your child talk more. You point, label objects, and ask questions. Children's oral language skills improved, one study found, after fifteen weeks of this interactive style of reading.

The Stony Brook Reading and Language Project, led by researcher Grover Whitehurst, developed the "PEER sequence" to summarize the fairly natural and brief exchange:

- **PROMPT your child to say something about the book:** "What is this?" (pointing to bird)
- **EVALUATE your child's response:** (child says "bird") "That's right!"
- **EXPAND on your child's response** by rephrasing it or adding information to it: "It's a blackbird."
- **REPEAT a prompt about the expansion:** "Can you say blackbird?"

When baby first starts talking, ask him to name objects. "What is that?"

Later, ask what, when, where, and why prompts: "When does the moon come out?" "Where are all the animals going?" "What is that sneaky gorilla doing?"

As your child is able to answer those, ask open-ended questions: "What's happening in this picture?"

You want to use the PEER sequence on almost every page, Whitehurst says, after you've read through the book once or twice.

≫

TRY THIS

Find a picture book with few words. For example, in Good Night, Gorilla, *each page says little more than "Good night." * Flotsam *has no words at all. Without a written narrative to fall back on, you have to make up a story based on the pictures.*

1½ years–3 years

Read alphabet books and rhymes. Both teach children about phonemes, the sounds of letters. Choose alphabet books that show several things starting with the same letter ("C is a crab with two clamping claws") and rhyming books ("Today I say! Without delay!"). As you're reading, pause so that your child can finish the sentence: "And the noisy, nasty nuisance grew, 'til the villagers cried ___ [What can we do?]"

Sound out words, syllable by syllable. This helps children link letters and their sounds, necessary for decoding words and for spelling. At this stage, your child learns to name a letter and make the sound of that letter, can tell you a word that rhymes with another word, and knows you've said "cat" if you make the sounds /k/ and /at/.

4–5 years

Have your child read aloud. Give explicit feedback and guidance along the way. This significantly improves word recognition, fluency, and comprehension—both for good and not-so-good readers, and across ages.

Relate an event in the story to real life: "We saw a boat yesterday, didn't we?" "Remember the last time you got frustrated like that?"

Ask questions about the story while you read. Reread parts that your child didn't understand. After the story—or before reading it yet again—ask a question about the plot: "Did Franklin want a dog for a pet? How did his parents react?" Have your child come up with his own questions about the story. Research hints that the conversation during reading is more important than the actual reading.

WHY READ

Reading isn't just pleasurable, it's necessary. It opens our minds to new ideas and possibilities; it informs and, sometimes, it inspires. It's a lovely way for you and your child to bond with each other.

Reading also presents by far the best opportunity to learn new words. We're not all that expansive when we talk. Children's books tend to use almost twice as many unusual words as college-educated adults do in conversation. A larger vocabulary helps children with schoolwork because they can spend more time understanding what they're reading and less time decoding the words they're reading.

The path to raising an avid reader—a fifth grader who reads twenty minutes a day outside of school versus the average of five minutes a day—is lots of talking and reading with your children. But among parents whose youngest child is 5 or younger, only 60 percent read with their children every day. It's hard to do if you work full-time or have more than one child, parents report.

One good way to make time? Turn off the TV (see page 140).

Say, "You worked so hard!"

When our kids impress us, our praise falls into one of several categories:

1. "Good running!" (praise that focuses on effort, strategies, or actions)
2. "You're a great runner." (praise that focuses on personal traits)
3. "Wow!" (any other type of positive encouragement)

Which one will most encourage your child to love learning, relish a challenge, and work harder in school? Number 1, called "process praise." It matters even when baby is just a year old.

Why some kids persevere

Carol Dweck of Stanford has been studying motivation and perseverance since the 1960s. "Why do some students give up when they encounter difficulty, whereas others who are no more skilled continue to strive and learn?" she wondered in an article in *Scientific American*.

It depends, she discovered, on the students' beliefs about *why* they failed: why they didn't get this math problem right or perform that piano piece well. And the way children are praised has a profound role in creating those beliefs.

Children fall into one of two categories:

- Those with a fixed mindset, who believe their successes are a result of their innate talent or smarts
- Those with a growth mindset, who believe their successes are a result of their hard work

Fixed mindset

Kids with a fixed mindset believe that you are stuck with however much intelligence you're born with. They would agree with this statement: "If you have to work hard, you don't have ability. If you have ability, things come naturally to you." When they fail, these kids feel trapped. They start thinking they must not be as talented or smart as everyone's been telling them. They avoid challenges, fearful that they won't look smart.

What creates a fixed mindset? Praising personal traits, or "person praise."

Growth mindset

Kids with a growth mindset believe that intelligence can be cultivated: the more learning you do, the smarter you become. These kids understand that even geniuses must work hard. When they suffer a setback, they believe they can improve by putting in more time and effort. They value learning over looking smart. They persevere through difficult tasks.

What ushers kids into a growth mindset? Process praise.

Mindsets form early

Even 4-year-olds have settled into one of these two mindsets. In her book *Mindset*, Dweck writes about an experiment she conducted:

> We offered four-year-olds a choice: They could redo an easy jigsaw puzzle or they could try a harder one. Even at this tender age, children with the fixed mindset—the ones who believed in fixed traits—stuck with the safe one. Kids who are born smart "don't make mistakes," they told us.

As you might imagine, either view of themselves profoundly affects kids' success as they progress through school and through life.

> **GOOD TO KNOW**

As toddlers, boys hear process praise more frequently than girls. Twenty-four percent of the praise boys hear is process praise. For girls, it's 10 percent.

In kids' own words

Fixed mindset	Growth mindset
"The main thing I want when I do my schoolwork is to show how good I am at it."	"It's much more important for me to learn things in my classes than it is to get the best grades."
"To tell the truth, when I work hard at my schoolwork, it makes me feel like I'm not very smart."	"The harder you work at something, the better you'll be at it."
"I would try not to take this subject ever again."	"I would work harder in this class from now on."

Henry (3) & Hope

Where do kids' mindsets come from?

Stanford researcher Carol Dweck gathered up fifth graders, randomly divided them in two groups, and had them work on problems from an IQ test. She then told the first group:

"Wow, that's a really good score. You must be smart at this."

She told the second group:

"Wow, that's a really good score. You must have tried really hard."

She continued to test the kids. Kids praised for their effort were more likely to take the more challenging task when presented a choice. They were more likely to continue feeling motivated to learn, and to retain their confidence as problems got harder.

Kids praised for their intelligence requested the easier task, lost their confidence as problems got harder, and were much more likely to inflate their test scores when recounting them.

Later, Dweck and her colleagues took the study out of the lab and into the home. Every four months for two years, Stanford and University of Chicago researchers visited fifty-three families and recorded them for ninety minutes as they went about their usual routines. The children were 14 months old at the start of the study.

Researchers then calculated the percentages of process praise, person praise, and other praise parents used. (Parents were told they were participating in a study of child language development, not praise specifically.)

Five years went by. Then the researchers surveyed the children, now 7 to 8 years old, on their attitudes toward challenges and learning. An example: "How much would you like to do mazes that are very hard so you can learn more about doing mazes?" Children with a growth mindset tended to be more interested in challenges.

Which kids had a growth mindset? Those who had heard more process praise as toddlers.

Two ways to plant a growth mindset

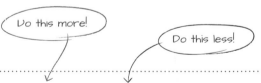

Praise effort

Personally, I find that praising effort takes effort. My reflexive first thought upon witnessing an impressive baby act is to give person praise: "Wow, you're so good at that!" (Even if I wish she weren't quite so good at that. As in, "Wow, how did you climb up onto the toilet, pull yourself over to the counter, sit down with your feet in the sink, turn on the faucet, and help yourself to a little soap?")

I'm not alone. About 85 percent of parents with young children Dweck surveyed agreed with this statement: "It is necessary to praise children's ability when they perform well on a task to make them feel that they are smart." Dweck thinks this sentiment might be why most parents, even those who have a growth mindset themselves, tend to give "person praise."

So repeat after me: praise effort, not ability.

Give brain lessons

Teach your child that the brain is like a muscle: the more you use it, the stronger it gets. The way you exercise it is by practicing skills and learning new things.

It's never too late to rewire the brain. Middle-schoolers and college students with fixed mindsets were able to improve academically when they were taught this lesson.

	Praising the process	**Praising the person**
Toddlers	"Good running!"	"You're so good at that!"
	"Good try."	"You're so smart."
	"I like how you covered your mouth."	"Good girl." / "Big boy."
	"You did a good job drawing."	"You're a good artist."
School-age	"You worked so hard!"	"You're so smart."
	"That seemed easy for you; let's work on something more challenging."	"You're so talented at this."
	"I like the way you approached that problem."	"Wow, you got an A without even studying."

Other praise: Praise that doesn't fit into these categories—like "Wow!" or "You got it!"—isn't shown to affect mindset, but it's still positive encouragement.

Quotes from Dweck's studies

Teach sign language

Wouldn't it be nice if baby could tell you his needs before he's able to talk? Oh, but he can.

First, you learn a handful of signs relevant to baby. For example, the sign for "milk" looks like squeezing a cow udder. "More" is tapping the tips of all fingers and thumbs together. Then you train baby to sign them, too.

This way, your baby can communicate his needs to you months before he can verbalize them. Or he can help you understand what he's so cutely but indecipherably talking about.

A lot less frustration

As you might imagine, being able to communicate (and be understood) vastly cuts down on baby's crying and whining.

Researchers think signing helps prevent the behavior problems connected with language delays, particularly among children with developmental delays or sensory impairments.

Some parents have heard that learning to sign will delay baby's speech, but there's no evidence to support that notion.

Two ways to teach baby

Friends and I took a baby signing class together. We learned dozens of signs: for foods and animals, "mama" and "papa," "hot" and "cold," "hungry" and "thirsty," "more" and "all done," "play" and "sleep," "hurt" and "where," "please" and "thank you."

It's possible for a baby as young as 6 months old to sign after about six weeks of training. Our babies weren't that quick. Maybe that's because we just made the signs whenever we said the corresponding words—more "something we

do for fun" than "training." To teach baby the way researchers do, you'd employ operant-conditioning theory. Fancy. It works like this:

Say it's snack time and you bust out pieces of pear. Give one to baby and make the sign for "pear." Then follow these steps:

1. Hold up another piece of pear and wait five seconds for him to make the sign.
2. If he doesn't, make the sign yourself. Again wait five seconds for him to make the sign.
3. If he doesn't, use his fingers to form the sign. Give him the pear. Make the sign yourself.
4. Repeat. (Researchers do this for a five-minute session several times a day.)

If at any point baby makes the sign himself, he gets the pear and a "Yes! That's right: pear!"

As soon as baby occasionally makes the sign within five seconds, increase the delay to ten seconds. Then twenty seconds. This progressive delay is only for step 1. Step 2 stays at five seconds: once you model the sign, help baby make the sign five seconds later.

I didn't get *that* formal about teaching baby sign language. But my laid-back method, which took closer to four months, still worked. I must say, it was pretty cool when my baby signed for "milk" or "potty" before she could say the words. And I loved being able to direct baby to sign "please" instead of whining "unh! unh! unh!" when she felt the desperate need to pick the blueberries out of my oatmeal.

Bigger vocabulary, better memory

Several decades of research on sign language point to benefits for children with normal hearing. In multiple studies, kids in preschool, kindergarten, or first grade studied American Sign Language for one academic year. The results are intriguing:

A leap in vocabulary. Kindergartners jumped to the equivalent of a second-grade vocabulary.

Better readers. Kindergartners scored higher on reading placement tests.

Kids remember the words longer. Preschoolers' short-term memory was slightly better.

Kids learn ASL quickly and easily. A language that uses gestures and visuals works well for young children, whose control over their hands and eyes develops faster than control over their voice and speech.

Visual-spatial cognition improves. These are the processes we use in identifying an object visually, pattern matching, making mental representations, and in rotation and orientation—skills an engineer or architect would use.

Kids love it. They're enthusiastic about learning, asking for more signs. (They're also better behaved in the classroom, teachers report, because the kids must pay attention.)

The benefits last. Gains in vocabulary were still evident three years later, even though the kids hadn't taken further ASL lessons.

TRY THIS

- *Start by learning the signs you'll use most with baby; don't dive in to the overwhelming task of learning an entire language.*

- *Sign in as many situations as you're able. Our teacher wanted us to aim for regularly using a dozen signs in the first month.*

- *Combine signs as often as you can: "Eat more pasta?" instead of just "pasta."*

- *Be patient. It takes seemingly forever for baby to start signing, so it's easy to give up or stress about it.*

- *Watch for baby's personalized version of your signs. (My baby's version of "please" was to put both hands on her belly and swipe them to her sides, rather than the proper sign, which is to circle one hand at her chest.)*

WHERE TO LEARN SIGNS FOR BABY

- Take a class at your library or community center.
- *Sign with Your Baby*, by researcher Joseph Garcia, is one popular DVD program based on American Sign Language.
- Sign2Me makes a CD of catchy songs called "Li'l Pick Me Up!" that help you remember signs. (My favorites: "More Milk," "Please Change My Diaper," "Sometimes When I Am Hungry," and "I Said 'Oww!'")
- ASL University's "First 100 Signs" are good for baby: lifeprint.com

Plan playdates in a second language

Parents who want to raise a bilingual baby find that,
despite their best intentions, the job is not so clear-cut.

The most common approaches include "one parent, one language" (mom speaks her native language to baby, and dad does the same) and "home/community" (parents speak one language at home, even if that's not both parents' first language, and baby picks up the second language outside the home).

Both strategies ensure that baby understands a second language. But the child often declines to *speak* the second language. The key?

Reinforce that language beyond the family, says researcher François Grosjean. Get help from babysitters, library story times, community events, immersion preschools—and especially playdates.

That's because, to bother retaining a language, kids need to see a clear use for it. Friends who speak that language present a very good reason.

Social interaction triggers learning

Researcher Patricia Kuhl, at the University of Washington, wondered if 9-month-old babies could learn a language they'd never heard. The babies, whose parents spoke only English, read books and played with Mandarin speakers three times a week, for twenty-five minutes at a time, over four weeks. Then Kuhl used noninvasive imaging technology to assess the babies' brain activity as they heard Mandarin sounds. For at least a month afterward, the babies were as good at picking out the vowel and consonant sounds of Mandarin as babies born in Taiwan.

But only if the babies heard the language from a real-live human being. Presented with TV or an audiotape in Mandarin, babies didn't learn a thing. Beyond age 2, kids are better able to learn from screens (see page 140), though social interaction is still best.

Being bilingual benefits baby

Parents often fear that learning multiple languages will delay baby's language skills, but there's no evidence to support that notion. Monolingual and bilingual children both hit language milestones within the expected range, studies show. It's also natural for a bilingual baby to alternate between languages in one sentence. Called "code-switching," it's not a sign of language delay or confusion.

Rather, being bilingual is good for baby's brain. Compared with monolingual babies, bilingual babies

- **stay open to learning longer.** Their brains are still able to detect the contrasting sounds of languages at 10 to 12 months old, past the usual window of 8 to 10 months old.
- **are better at switching mental gears.** When we hear the beginnings of a word, our brains immediately begin guessing at the rest of the word. For bilinguals, both languages are activated each time they hear a word. Constantly switching between languages gives the babies a cognitive

≫

workout. All that practice improves the brain's ability to monitor its environment and to switch between sets of rules in situations unrelated to language. For example, in one study of bilingual and monolingual 7-month-olds, researchers played a sound that cued the arrival of a puppet, which appeared on one side of a screen. When they heard the sound, both groups of babies soon looked to that spot on the screen in anticipation. Then the puppet began appearing on the other side of the screen. The bilingual babies quickly switched to looking in anticipation at the new location. The monolingual babies didn't.

- **are more creative.** When asked to draw a fantastical flower, bilingual 4- and 5-year-olds drew hybrids like a kite flower, while monolingual kids drew flowers missing petals or leaves.
- **are more accurate and more efficient at tasks testing executive function.** Children were asked to reproduce patterns of colored blocks, repeat a series of numbers out loud, define words, and solve math problems in their heads. The bilingual children were "significantly more successful." These mental puzzles test a suite of skills called executive functions, which allow us to plan and prioritize (see page 106).

One language for you, two for baby?

If you're not bilingual, but hoping to raise a baby who is, one approach is to find a nanny who will speak only that language to baby. If that means *you're* unable to readily communicate with the nanny, translate.google.com comes in handy, along with the occasional translation from a friend. Learn at least a little of the language yourself. (I don't know very much Mandarin, but I'm glad that I know baby's plea for *lán méi* means blueberries.) Then plan those playdates.

There's no good guideline for how much exposure is "enough." For one thing, it's nearly impossible for parents to estimate for a researcher how many minutes of each language their child hears in a day. But clarifying your own goals for baby—fluency, or just exposure—will help guide your approach.

Researchers do know it's best to start early. Up to age 7, children are able to achieve fluency in a second language similar to that of a native speaker. After age 7, the level of fluency one can achieve takes a serious dive. Of course, people do learn languages later in life, but via different brain mechanisms and with a lower level of fluency.

GOOD TO KNOW

Bilingual families say it's harder than they expected to be consistent about speaking only one language to baby. A parent may feel more comfortable talking about work in English and talking about leisure in Spanish, and so switch between the two. If friends are over for dinner and all speaking one language, both parents will speak it. As always, there's theory and then there's practice. You have to do what works for you.

Sleep, eat & potty

Yes, baby has to be taught how to do everything.
A healthy sense of humor helps.

Opal & Zoey (9 days)

Guard your sleep

It sounds so simple: just sleep when the baby sleeps!

Well, it's not easy—you have so many things you want to do and no other time to do them—but it's pretty much your only option. Getting a decent amount of sleep might save your job and your marriage, not to mention your sanity.

Sleep deprivation sucks

- Sleep loss hurts a range of cognitive abilities: your ability to regulate strong emotions, to find the right word to communicate, to see someone else's perspective, to hold things in your memory, to react quickly. This starts happening after only two weeks of getting six hours of sleep per night.
- Couples are more often hostile toward each other after baby arrives, making it harder to create an emotionally stable home environment (see page 22).
- Chronic sleep loss and depression are closely related.

Drop everything

The moment baby arrives, let go of checking your e-mail, running your errands, working on your hobbies, watching your TV shows, posting frequently online, and pretty much everything else in your previous life. In the early weeks, focus on feeding your baby, getting sleep, and letting your body heal. Other things can come later. If your partner can't take a leave from work, find a relative or friend who can come stay with you, to focus on caring for you and managing the house while you recover. Yes, you need to be taken care of right now, too.

Go to bed (gasp!) early

No matter how late you stay up, baby is probably going to get up at the same time each morning. So do the math. If baby generally wakes at 6:00 a.m., and is up ninety minutes at night, and you do best on eight hours of sleep, get yourself to bed by 8:30 p.m. "But," you argue, "how will I get this or that done? How will I get any 'me' time?" You won't. Sleep is more important right now.

If possible, stagger bedtimes with your partner and share middle-of-the-night duties. In the morning, baby generally will want to nap ninety minutes after waking, and perhaps you should, too. As needed, have someone—family, friend, neighbor, postpartum doula, babysitter—watch the baby while you catch up on sleep. They say it takes a village. That starts now.

> **TRY THIS**
>
> *In the first weeks, go to bed early and don't get up—meaning, don't shower and get dressed and decide you're up for the day— until you've accumulated eight hours of sleep.*

Sarah, mother of twins Opal & Zoey (9 days)

Guard baby's sleep, too

Sleep is vital. Well-rested babies are better able to consolidate memory, to focus, and to adapt. They're less easily frustrated, less irritable, and less fussy.

One of the best things you can do right from the start is to not keep baby up too long during the day. New parents inadvertently do this by missing (or ignoring) baby's sleepy signs and keeping baby in an environment that's too stimulating.

Unfortunately, babies don't fall asleep just because they're tired. The biorhythm that governs our wake-sleep cycles only reduces alertness; it doesn't force sleep. So help baby out: create favorable conditions (low light, soothing, a bed or a walk) at favorable times (when baby is sleepy).

Find baby's timing
Newborns aren't awake much, but when they are, it shouldn't be for more than forty-five minutes at a time. From 6 weeks to 6 months old, baby wants to stay awake ninety minutes or so (it can vary by thirty minutes in either direction). Then, through 1 year old, the window gradually increases to three hours.

To find your baby's timing, look for sleepy signs: rubbing eyes or ears, staring off into middle distance, becoming less coordinated, or getting more fussy. If you see your baby's signs, help baby sleep. Some babies are good at propping their eyelids open; if so, a meltdown is a sure sign baby needed to sleep.

Awake times lengthen as the brain matures, and as environmental cues (like daylight) and social cues (like your family's daily rhythm) weigh in.

Other tips for timing
Only fools rush in. New parents often come running at baby's first noise during a nap. But babies spend the first twenty to forty minutes in "active sleep," before falling into a deeper "quiet sleep" for about sixty minutes. In active sleep, babies might sigh, cry a little, jerk limbs, or even open their eyes. They wake more easily during active sleep. Baby may fall back asleep—or stay asleep—if you just hang back and listen instead of going in to check. Don't be in a rush to move baby, either, during active sleep. If baby falls asleep on the boob, or while bouncing with dad, keep it up until baby is in quiet sleep. Then transfer baby into bed. After all that work soothing baby to sleep, you *really* don't want her popping awake the second she hits the crib. (Ask me how I know.)

Help baby transition. After one cycle of active sleep plus quiet sleep, baby either wakes or starts another cycle. Some babies easily transition between active and quiet sleep (likely the babies we think of as "good sleepers"). Some don't. If baby wakes up too quickly from a nap, try soothing him back to sleep.

Let go. If helping baby fall asleep for naps is a huge struggle, give up after twenty or thirty minutes. Your timing was just off. I went through this obsessive phase when our daughter was 4 months old, trying for far too long to get naps. It was exhausting. I don't recommend it.

Don't skip naps or push out bedtime. After three months, baby's sleep schedule becomes more organized. Many babies, mine included, want to wake up around 6:00 a.m. no matter what time they went to bed. (Thank goodness my husband does, too.) Don't skip baby's naps, or move bedtime back, trying to get baby to sleep in. All that does is create an overtired baby. It may seem counterintuitive, but for babies, less sleep today doesn't mean more sleep tonight.

> **GOOD TO KNOW**
>
> *Infants tend to nap ninety minutes after waking up, even if they just slept all night.*

Help baby sleep better at night

Babies take months to regulate their sleep, but you can help give baby the right idea.

Give baby clues about night and day. Newborns sleep (and eat and poop) throughout a twenty-four-hour period. They don't know night from day. Sorry! Baby will need your help with feeding and soothing every couple of hours, as baby focuses on getting enough food into that tiny tummy and regulating internal systems, which used to be regulated by mom's body. This takes about three months. On the plus side, there's no point getting all anxious at this stage about schedules, nap lengths, and whether baby is sleeping through the night.

You can help baby construct his internal clock by exposing him to bright light, noise, and activity during the day, and darkness, quiet, and calm at night.

Sleep in the same room as baby at night. Sleeping near your newborn helps regulate baby's breathing, temperature, and stress levels. It makes breastfeeding easier, because mom and baby's light and deep sleep rhythms sync up. Plus, in the beginning, you're going to constantly check that baby is still alive—might as well do it by opening one eye rather than by getting out of bed.

Probably the easiest way to sleep near baby is a co-sleeper, which is a three-sided crib placed flush against your bed, with both mattresses at about the same level. Co-sleeping is simpler than sharing a bed, which in the West requires some dramatic modifications to be safe.

Bed-sharing requires a firm mattress on the floor by itself, away from walls and furniture that could trap baby, with no loose sheets, blankets, or pillows that could smother baby. Only the mother, who must be sober and a nonsmoker, shares the bed with baby. Bed-sharing means more frequent wakings for both mom and baby, but it may feel right for you. Or it may be the only way baby will sleep. New moms tend to readily fall back asleep after waking; thank you, hormones. But consider transitioning baby to her own bed after a few months. Bed-sharing interrupts and shortens baby's quiet-sleep phase, studies show.

There are other options for beds, given that, after the coziness of the womb, most newborns don't love to lay flat on a big mattress. Some parents use a baby swing. Legendary Seattle doula Penny Simkin likes the Fisher-Price Rock 'n Play. Both have an inclined back and sloped sides, which make baby feel cozy. The incline also can help if baby has reflux. The Rock 'n Play is small enough to fit next to your bed, and it's lightweight enough to pull around—great for containing baby in a visible place while you do things like shower and eat. Before six months, you transition baby to a crib.

Whichever setup works best for you, definitely sleep in the same room as baby for the first three months. Baby needs more babying during this "fourth trimester." It does mean giving up some privacy as a couple, but you can find that in other ways.

Swaddle for better sleep. A swaddling blanket snugly wraps baby's arms straight against his sides. This helps baby sleep longer; without it, his arms randomly startle during sleep, potentially waking him up. Swaddling also makes baby more comfortable with sleeping on his back. Newborns must be put to sleep on their backs to reduce the risk of sudden infant death syndrome, or SIDS.

Newborns often protest swaddling at first, because in the womb they're used to having their hands near their mouths. So you might think, "My baby hates this thing; forget it." Not so fast! Finish swaddling, and then immediately comfort baby: nurse, or walk while patting the bum and shhh-shhh-shhh-ing. (This was my doula's tip for introducing baby to slings, wraps, or buckle carriers, too.)

Some babies (and parents) fuss at one type of swaddle but like another. Options:

- **Velcro designs,** such as the SwaddleMe and Halo SleepSack. These are easy for you to get on, but easy for some babies to get off.

- **A large, thin blanket, the most versatile option.** You can swaddle baby arms bent or straight; you can create a divot between the legs if baby will be strapped into a seat. They double as regular blankets and spit-up cloths. Aden + Anais makes the best blankets; most receiving blankets are too small or bulky. The technique you want is the double swaddle. (Look it up to see a video.) This involves using a second blanket or a Swaddle Strap to secure the arms inside a traditional swaddle.
- **The Miracle Blanket,** a premade double swaddle. No way baby can bust out of that thing.

Whichever blanket you choose, your swaddling technique must allow baby to move his hips, to prevent hip dysplasia, and to take a deep breath. The arms are what must be snug. Practice on a doll—or sleeping baby, if you dare—to get the hang of it.

Create a bedtime routine. Sometime after baby settles into a discernable sleep pattern, around 4 months old, do the same things in the same order at the same time, every night before bed. This creates predictability for baby and signals it's time to wind down. After three weeks of a consistent routine, moms in one study reported that babies were falling asleep more quickly, staying asleep longer, and waking up fewer times during the night. Moms' moods improved, too.

Make bedtime daddy time. After six months, baby no longer *needs* food during the night. So, to help set baby's internal clock, encourage baby to feed more during the day by gradually reducing nursing time or bottle amounts at night. If baby wakes up, dad can go in for one minute to soothe. Keep the soothing quiet, low-key, and in the dark. It also often takes far less time for dad to put baby to bed at night than for mom. Something about the lack of breasts . . .

Around 6 months old, move up bedtime. As soon as baby drops the third nap, move up bedtime. Otherwise, baby won't get enough sleep overnight. My husband and I had to play around with this to find the right time. We put baby to bed fifteen or thirty minutes earlier each night, so long as she continued to wake for the day at 6:00 a.m. If she woke up earlier than usual or took longer to fall asleep than usual, we knew the bedtime was too early. We settled on a bedtime between 6:30 and 7:00 p.m., which was awesome for getting some time to ourselves in the evenings.

Get outside. Babies who slept better at night were exposed to significantly more blue-spectrum light between noon and 4 p.m.

Get help. Solid resources include *The Happiest Baby on the Block* by Harvey Karp and troublesometots.com by Alexis Dubief. Don't get sucked into reading all the books and blogs. They contradict each other, so it's just confusing. If you do have strong instincts for what to do, go with those.

> **GOOD TO KNOW**
>
> *By 4 months old, 85 percent of babies sleep for at least a five-hour stretch, a study using time-lapse video showed. But 15 percent don't. By 1 year old, 73 percent of babies sleep between 10:00 p.m. and 6:00 a.m. But 27 percent don't. On top of that, all babies go through developmental phases that interrupt their previous (sterling, or tolerable, or at least predictable) sleep habits.*
>
> *So, prepare for a long haul. Your expectations surrounding sleep will color whether you view parenting as stressful.*

Give baby chances to self-soothe

Most babies need help learning how to fall asleep or fall back to sleep on their own.

I've seen, with my own eyes, babies who just close their eyes and drift off to sleep when you lay them in bed. (OK, one baby.) Our newborn? She cried. Like many parents, we soothed baby to sleep by any means necessary: Harvey Karp's Five S's, nursing, walks in the carrier, bouncing on the exercise ball. Then we'd wait until she was in "quiet sleep," lay her down and tiptoe away. If that's you, around six months, start letting baby fall asleep with gradually less attention.

Studies show it helps if you

- wait a bit before you respond to awakenings,
- put baby to bed sleepy but not 100 percent asleep, and
- put baby in his own room.

This is scary because it means changing what you know works. Easygoing babies may not mind the change. Others will mind—and let you know about it.

One method is to soothe baby for gradually less time before walking out, coming back in if baby cries and doing it again. All the back and forth can feel like this is not working. But it is. The purpose is giving baby *chances* to self-soothe, letting him practice.

Similarly, if you usually go to baby the moment he cries in the middle of the night, wait a few minutes before you go in. See if the cry escalates or not. Give baby another chance to self-soothe.

Moving baby's bed to a separate room can help because you're not aware of and responding to every night waking. And when baby wakes up, he doesn't think, "Hey, I see you *right there*. How about a little assistance?" But even if you want to keep baby's crib in your room a while longer, get going on those other two bullet points.

Why start this tough process around six months? Because baby has settled from a big developmental leap around four months. After eight months, baby makes another big leap: a fuller understanding of "object permanence." (Though some researchers think it happens at three or four months.)

That means baby can remember whether you were there when she fell asleep. It's disconcerting to her if conditions aren't the same when she wakes up throughout the night. She cries for you to come back and re-create the proper conditions. A pacifier (apt to fall out of baby's mouth), or a sound machine on a timer, can cause the same trouble.

So at six months, you have a relatively stable developmental window to work with. But this timing is just an ideal. In reality, your baby's developmental leaps might come at slightly different times. On top of that, there's always a tooth coming in, a cold, or a growth spurt to contend with.

Even if you're not feeling desperate for decent sleep, don't put off supporting baby's ability to self-soothe. If you do, studies hint, baby may begin to lose the ability.

THE RESEARCH

Eighty babies were videotaped sleeping at 1, 3, 6, 9, and 12 months old. The study was led by Melissa Burnham and Thomas Anders at the University of California–Davis. As you might expect, most of the babies became better at self-soothing over time, as they matured. But 40 percent became worse at self-soothing over time. The babies who lost their self-soothing abilities tended to be put to bed after they were already asleep. They slept in their parents' rooms, and they didn't have a "lovie" to cuddle.

Jess & Naomi (14 months)

CAN I HAVE A DO-OVER?

We thought we had the self-soothing thing down. Bedtime seemed easy; baby slept well. But then it came time to transfer baby to a crib. Oh, baby screamed at that crib. As soon as we'd lay her down, she'd pull herself up to standing in the crib and cry.

I wished we'd transitioned baby to the crib earlier, when she still fit in her Rock 'n Play bed. Then we could have more gradually introduced her to the crib: letting her play in it each day until she was comfortable; then trying for naps; then trying for overnight sleep. But that was a moot point.

What worked best was a little extra TLC that supported baby's self-soothing abilities—unlike my initial idea to nurse her to sleep. My husband would hold baby on his shoulder, walking and singing until her body relaxed. He'd lay her down in bed not quite asleep. Then he'd place his hand on her tummy, gently holding her in place, and shhhhh until she relaxed again. Then he'd walk out, still shhhhh-ing.

Still, baby was waking up through the night. With her crib in our room, it was easy for her to request our assistance falling back asleep. She'd stand up and cry. I practiced with baby during the day on getting back down to the mattress. She got it. But at night, she'd repeatedly squat and reach for the mattress, then change her mind. (Agh, so close!) Desperate, we veered from sleep book to sleep book. We tried laying baby down again and again, hoping she wouldn't bother to stand up again. (This would go on for more than an hour; she'd win.) We tried lying on the floor, patting the crib mattress for so long we'd practically fall asleep. (Is that being consistent or just stupid?)

After two months of nightly struggles, at 9 months old, we gave up. We moved baby to her own room to cry it out. We gave her a tour of her new surroundings and told her if she needed to cry a little, it was OK, but we'd open the door in the morning. We braced ourselves for rounds of heartbreaking crying.

Not one peep! She instantly slept through the night. It almost seemed like *we'd* been the ones keeping *her* up.

Crying it out, for a time, is fine

If you're utterly exhausted from sleep deprivation, you may begin to ask: When will this baby sleep through the $@%! night? And how do I make that happen right $@%! now?

You may begin to read every single book and forum post in existence about how to get your baby to sleep through the night. And your head may begin to spin.

One of the most controversial methods of sleep training is leaving baby alone and letting her cry herself to sleep. Battle lines are drawn between those who are certain it will scar baby for life and those who swear it's the only thing that worked to get everyone a full night's sleep.

A long-term study says baby will be fine.

Researchers from Australia and the United Kingdom, led by Anna Price, studied several hundred babies 8 months old. (It's generally accepted that you shouldn't try sleep training before 6 months old.)

The researcher studied two versions of crying it out:

Controlled crying
You briefly—as in, less than a minute—comfort baby with a back rub and some gentle words that she probably can't hear through her crying, then leave the room and close the door for three minutes. Repeat, staying away for five minutes. Then ten minutes. Cap it at ten. Incrementally, over a week, increase baby's time alone. (See the schedule in *Solve Your Child's Sleep Problems* by Richard Ferber.)

Camping out/fading
You sit near baby's bed and try to soothe with your voice, such as singing a song, until baby is asleep. Each night over three weeks, you move your chair incrementally farther away, until it's out the door.

The study did not look at "unmodified extinction," in which baby is left to cry indefinitely. It works, but so do gentler methods. Researchers don't endorse it.

More sleep, less depression
Parents chose which method to use; some tried both. A control group tried neither. Short term, crying it out helped. At 10 months old, 56 percent of babies who cried it out had sleep problems, while 68 percent of controls had sleep problems. At 12 months old, it was 39 percent vs. 55 percent. After two years, fewer mothers were depressed: 15 percent vs. 26 percent.

At six years, the researchers followed up again. Were the kids who had cried it out as infants more stressed than the kids in the control group? How did their mental health, social skills, sleep problems, and relationship with their parents compare? What about the mother's depression, anxiety, and stress (which are linked to infant sleep)?

On every count: no difference.

The researchers didn't say parents *should* let baby cry it out. Not every parent has the stomach for it, given that every minute leaving baby to cry can feel like ten. The study says only that, if you want to try controlled crying or camping out, it can reduce sleep problems while doing no harm at this age.

Be consistent
Once you start, commit. Giving in randomly will cause baby to cling even more tightly to crying. Then, give it a week. This is hard because you want immediate results, and every day feels like a week. Plus, decisions made groggily at 2:00 a.m. aren't always the ones you intended. You might want to take notes for the week on what you're really doing at each night waking, so you can tell whether you're on your intended path—or just think you are.

Just when you think you've got bedtime figured out, something will change.

My husband and I struggled through this when our 22-month-old figured out how to open her bedroom door after we'd put her to bed. That meant a bleary-eyed baby was stumbling into the living room, making random requests: "Hungry. [Insert food she'd declined to eat at dinner]. Milk! I want to sleep with Mommy and Daddy. Listen to music? Ride my bicycle! I want to walk outside."

Naps were not happening; she wasn't sleeping through the night anymore. Round and round we'd go, baby repeatedly popping out of her room moments after we put her there. We tried various responses—gently returning her to bed again and again, more food, a stint on the potty, ignoring her, counting to three, holding the door closed—until I'd had it and would yell, "Get back in your bed!" and firmly dump her there. Which didn't work, either.

Finally, we started laying down on the floor next to baby's bed until she fell asleep. We were relieved to have found *something* that worked. But it was also disruptive to our own sleep, and it wasn't teaching her how to stay in bed on her own. We needed to step back and think. It was obvious that baby didn't need any of the food or toys she was requesting, and our attention just reinforced her behavior. We needed to stop providing that kind of attention. Maybe she didn't have the self-control to stay in her room now that she had gained the ability to get out. We needed to remove the option of opening the door. Maybe our bedtime routine—laying her down with a bottle and kissing her head—was too short, and bed felt like a place where she got left behind while we continued our evening.

New plan: we put a lock on the door (with baby's help). I let her test the handle to feel the difference between locked and unlocked. I told her she wouldn't be able to open the door when it was locked, and this would help her stay in her room at night. We would open the door in the morning.

We changed our bedtime routine, reading baby three stories as she lay in bed. My husband snuggled in close, so she'd get more cuddle time. Then we said good night. Baby immediately climbed out of bed. This time, we did our own version of "fading": we sat outside the door, instead of laying on her floor, to comfort her.

"I want Mommy to lay on the floor," she cried at the door. "Sad baby!"

"Aww, sad baby," I replied. "Yes, Mommy is right here on the floor. When we're sleepy, we lay down. Do you want to lay on the floor or climb into bed?" She wandered back to bed. We repeated this a few times. "I'm going to sing you a song, sweetie, to help you stay in bed," I said.

My song calmed her crying for a bit. When she cried again, I sang again. If she said, "I want Mommy to lay on the floor," I repeated, "Yes, I'm right here on the floor. I'll sing you a song."

This lasted for half an hour as she wandered between the door and her bed, crying off and on. "Get me OUT of here!" she said at one point. I tried not to laugh. I sang to her probably a half-dozen times as she woke up throughout the night. Each instance took less and less singing to calm her.

The next night, she stayed in bed from 7:30 p.m. to 6:30 a.m.—the usual. It's been a week. Bedtime is back on track.

I tell such a detailed story to make a few points. First, to solve the problem, we couldn't just be indignant that baby wasn't following our orders (although we were). We had to take a step back and try to figure out why baby might be doing this. Locking the door wasn't enough; I tried that for a couple of naps and was met with screeching. We also had to address what we guessed was baby's desire to spend more time with us or her sudden dislike of being left in bed.

Second, be willing to back out of an unsustainable solution, like laying on the floor was for us, and start over.

Third, give your new and improved plan a chance. Once we decided on our plan of empathizing and comforting from outside the door, we had to use it many times throughout the night. If we'd said after the first fifteen minutes, or after the first middle-of-the-night wakeup, "Well, she's still not staying in bed; that didn't work," we would have given up too soon.

Finally, you can see that baby is getting emotional support even though fading is a "cry it out" technique.

Preserve preschoolers' naps

Babies younger than 5 still benefit from a nap.

Naps aid learning. Researchers gave preschoolers a memory test in the morning and then a 2:00 p.m. nap. The preschoolers were tested again after the nap and also the next morning.

The children who napped scored higher on the memory test than non-nappers, both after the nap and the next day. Researchers swapped which children napped and which didn't. Same result.

Naps aid early learning, the researchers suggest, because kids' short-term memory is limited, and the sleep allows for more frequent memory consolidation.

Kids with regular bedtimes have better behavior. Whether bedtime was early or late, children with a regular bedtime had fewer behavioral problems, a British study found. (Only 20 percent of 3-year-olds and 9 percent of 5-year-olds in the study didn't have a regular bedtime.)

The longer the irregular bedtimes went on, the worse the behavioral problems were. But if those kids got onto a regular schedule by age 7, their behavior improved.

TRY THIS

Preschool teachers' secret: time the nap soon after lunch; have the kids lay down and stretch their legs, toes, hands, and arms; play soothing nature sounds; and rub the kids' backs for a bit.

If all else fails, your child can read in bed or play in her room for "quiet time."

GOOD TO KNOW

Ninety percent of kids get ten or eleven hours of sleep at night, studies show. Whichever amount is the norm for them, kids stick with it from age 2½ to 6. Kids tend not to make up for missed sleep, so it's important for them to get enough sleep each night. In one study, getting just an hour less sleep than needed increased the risk of low scores on a vocabulary test, leading the researchers to theorize that the sleep loss hurt language acquisition and memory.

Claire (3½)

Make bedtime less crazy

Older kids hear "Time for bed! Brush your teeth!" and somehow—is this universal?—it gets translated into "Run!"

So you're chasing them every step of the way. A routine chart halts the chase by creating very clear, consistent rules for bedtime.

Create a visual chart

The secret to an effective routine chart is to create it together with your kids. Your children gain some control over the process, and they're more enthusiastic about following a plan they've helped create. As kids get used to following the chart, which can take several weeks, hassles and power struggles begin to vanish.

1. **Brainstorm a list of the steps.** Sit down with your kids and ask them to tell you everything they need to get ready for bed. Take notes. Narrow it down to seven items or less (maybe only three for little kids, like "bath, jammies, story").
2. **Have your children illustrate each task.** They can draw pictures, or you can take pictures of them doing the task. Together, paste the pictures, in order, onto a poster. The chart doesn't need to have words or checkboxes. It doesn't need places for stickers; bribes and rewards create only short-term motivation. Make just a row or two of pictures that will remind your kids what to do next.
3. **Spend time training.** Focus on practicing one step per night, giving a little tutorial on each step. Return to the chart as soon as one task is done. Discuss consequences in advance: "Lights out is at 8:00 p.m. If you choose not to finish our steps, I will be putting you into bed the way you are— no cuddling, no story time—and closing the door."
4. **Let the routine chart be the boss.** When the kids get off task (intentionally or not), direct them to the chart rather than telling them what to do: "What's next on your routine chart?" "What needs to happen next so that we can get to story time?" "As soon as ___, then ___." "What did we agree was the next step in our bedtime routine?" For kids younger than 5, do the tasks along with them.

If your child still resists? Calmly point, lead, or carry him to the chart, and ask again. Or remind him that story time is coming once he brushes his teeth. Or say, "I'll be in your bedroom. Come find me when you're ready to put on your pajamas."

TRY THIS

Make bedtime more crazy!

The Natkin family found that evenings went more smoothly when they added five minutes for everyone to get crazy together—dance party! tickle fest!—before settling down for bed.

If bedtime is still a constant struggle after using your routine chart, parent coach Sarina Natkin says, ask yourself what piece is missing. Do the kids need more time with you? More control over the process?

If your child is constantly popping out of bed with requests, add those items to your routine: "Let's make sure you have everything you need before bed." Or try "bedtime tickets": kids can use two tickets per night to make requests. Any additional request is ignored, and the child is gently but silently deposited back in bed.

Whenever a plan isn't working, kick it back to your family meeting (see page 134) so that you can brainstorm solutions.

Tracy & Geneva (18 months)

Be laid-back about breastfeeding

Like the rest of parenting, breastfeeding is both rewarding and hard work. A relaxed attitude goes a long way.

Sixty percent of women want to breastfeed exclusively. But two-thirds of those women give up, studies show. Why? Women cited breastfeeding pain, worry that they weren't producing enough milk, and problems getting baby to latch. Expect that you'll experience these common issues, too. But trust that the right support can help you through.

Comfort is key

The first thing to know is: get comfortable. If you're not comfortable, adjust your body or baby's body. If your nipples are killing you, unlatch baby and try again. Breastfeeding your baby isn't supposed to cause searing pain in your neck, wrists, or nipples.

Start with the laid-back breastfeeding position. (One lactation consultant joked that if everyone used this technique, it would put her out of business.) Sit down, then scoot your hips forward and lean back, like you're slouching to watch TV. Place baby on her tummy against your chest, at any angle that's comfortable, and let her find your breast. It's easier for everything to fall into place than if you're sitting upright or lying down. Plus, you're supporting baby's body with your body instead of tiring out your arms. See biologicalnurturing.com for videos and more information.

Feed a calm baby

Practice when baby is calm rather than crying. It's easier for her to learn, and her tongue will be in the right place. Try to catch her hunger signs (rooting, hand to mouth) before she gets really upset. If she's upset, calm her first before you feed her.

Milk out = milk in

The more breast milk baby removes, the more breast milk you produce. So if your doctors tell you that baby needs formula, but you want to preserve the option of breastfeeding, you need to start pumping immediately. Work up to pumping at the highest setting you can stand, because (when things are working properly) babies remove more milk than pumps can.

Get support

Talk with your doctor about what happens right after labor. Your hospital might get you off to a good start. But it might not: only 7 percent of US hospitals are certified "baby-friendly," meaning they follow international guidelines for supporting new moms in breastfeeding. These hospitals initiate breastfeeding within the first hour after birth; place baby and mom together 24-7; encourage breastfeeding on demand, not on a schedule; and don't provide formula unless medically necessary. Even if your hospital isn't certified, you can request these accommodations of your doctor before you go into labor.

Get hands-on help. If your own mom is unable to teach you how to breastfeed, find a lactation consultant (ilca.org) or postpartum doula—preferably one who can come to your house—to show you the ropes.

Read _Breastfeeding Made Simple_ by Nancy Mohrbacher and Kathleen Kendall-Tackett. For problem solving, especially latch issues, have _The Ultimate Breastfeeding Book of Answers_ by Jack Newman on hand. The website kellymom.com is a huge resource as well.

Line up support from your partner, relatives, and friends. As soon as baby arrives, you'll need people to feed you, make sure your water bottle is constantly filled, and manage the house, while you focus on feeding baby and sleeping. New moms need care just as baby does. Women are incredibly vulnerable and in need of healing after giving birth. But in our society, women tend to expect themselves to quickly get back to cleaning, cooking, and exercising. If that's you, make an effort to counteract the tendency.

Make friends who share your ideas about breastfeeding. You can help each other become comfortable nursing in public, shrug off unsupportive comments from strangers or family, or stick with pumping (no one's favorite activity).

Some hospitals and community centers offer breastfeeding support groups.

THE RESEARCH

Breast is brainiest . . . by a little bit

Each month of breastfeeding adds a small gain, about one-third of a point, to your child's intelligence scores. Researchers from Harvard and Boston Children's Hospital studied data on more than thirteen hundred mothers and children. They adjusted for a host of factors, including socioeconomic status, the mother's intelligence, and whether baby was raised at home or in day care. The longer baby breastfeeds, they found, the higher baby's vocabulary scores at 3 years old and intelligence scores at 7 years old. A baby breastfed for twelve months would score four IQ points higher than a baby who was not breastfed. IQ does matter. But if breastfeeding just isn't working, there are plenty of other ways to help fulfill baby's intellectual potential.

GOOD TO KNOW

Breast milk isn't just food. Your body responds to baby's needs day to day by adjusting hormones, immune factors, volume of milk, sugars to feed the bacteria in baby's gut, and surely more properties that researchers haven't discovered yet.

"Eat food. Not too much. Mostly plants."

"My kid eats what I eat," you hear parents say, happy they're not preparing separate meals for their child.

For me, the reverse has turned out to be true. I found myself being so careful about feeding my baby healthy food, I realized *I* should eat more of what *baby* was eating.

Case in point: baby drinks a kale smoothie most days, an easy way to get her greens. (It tastes better than it sounds.)

Easier said than done

Food journalist Michael Pollan's advice—the title of this page—is based on the way humans ate for hundreds of thousands of years. Grasses, fruits, vegetables, small mammals, insects, and a distinct lack of sugar—this is the diet our brains and bodies function best on.

I've been working toward eating this way for fifteen years and counting. (Well, except for the insects.) If you're trying to do that, too, here are the things that have made it easier for me post-baby:

Buying fresh, local produce. Great-tasting food starts with high-quality ingredients. I'd heard that but didn't really know what it meant until I took a cooking class. We sampled organic carrots shipped to a big supermarket (dull, dense, bitter) and organic carrots freshly picked from a local farm (crisp, lively, sweet). The difference was a revelation.

Living in Seattle, I'm fortunate to have a farmers' market within walking distance and several options for community-supported agriculture programs. In a CSA program, you "subscribe" to a local farm each season in exchange for a box of produce delivered regularly. Our weekly box of produce is full of variety I never would have thought to buy on my own—delicata squash, eggplants, collard greens, kale, cabbage, sunchokes, beets.

Produce straight from the farm tastes *good*, even when you do very little to it.

A pressure cooker. I swear this thing should be issued to all new parents at the hospital. You can cook soups, barley risottos, beans, and curries in ten minutes instead of thirty to sixty minutes. These are mainly the meals we eat now.

A powerful blender. A high-end blender makes everything from smooth kale smoothies to broccoli pesto.

≫

Cooking in big batches once or twice a week. Cooking is not a hobby for me. I don't want to do it for every meal. So I aspire to make steel-cut oats, quinoa, roasted vegetables, and hearty soups to last the week. I may wash and chop ingredients one day and cook them the next.

Storing produce properly as soon as I bring it home. I admit, at times we've shoved our whole box of CSA produce into the fridge and promptly gone out for Thai food. My cooking plan works better when I put each item in plain view, so it gets used. And when I store each item properly, so it lasts longer.

Simple recipes. My criteria for a recipe: Does it have a minimal number of ingredients? Can I prep the ingredients one day and cook them the next? Will this freeze well if I triple the batch? Now we're talking.

I still can't get over how delicious and easy potato-leek soup is. You just cook four sliced leeks in a little butter until they're soft, add four cups of potato chunks and four cups of broth to the pot, keep cooking until the potatoes are tender, and then briefly blend the soup into a puree. That's four ingredients.

Make it taste good. Cook with fats, spices, and herbs. When we take pleasure in what we're eating, one study found, we absorb more of the nutrients from it.

So far, I've found great recipes at cookusinterruptus.com, nourishingmeals.com, and 101cookbooks.com. I credit smittenkitchen.com for building my confidence with recipes that just plain work.

Backups. I keep a Costco-sized box of Amy's lentil soup in the pantry for when I haven't had time to cook and it's "that kind of day." I also keep Lärabars, which have only a few ingredients, for snacks.

A kale smoothie every day. This is a great way to get raw greens. The fruit masks their taste, so "green juice," as baby calls it, goes down easy. Here's the recipe, adapted from nourishingmeals.com:

> 2 pieces of fruit (apple + pear, peach, or nectarine)
> 2 big bunches of greens, thick ribs removed (kale or chard + spinach or collard greens)
> 2 cups of cabbage, chopped
> 2 cups of water
> 1 lemon, juiced

Pulse the blender to chop everything, and puree until smooth. If it tastes too sweet, add more greens. If it tastes too green, add more fruit.

QUICK SNACKS THAT DON'T MAKE A MESS

- dried fruit, apple pieces, and walnuts
- fruit: berries (bought in bulk and frozen), bananas, grapes cut in half, or a mandarin orange
- pieces of broccoli, cauliflower, and carrots tossed in the microwave for two minutes, maybe with chunks of apple or yams. Or sweet potato, pear, and broccoli. Toss with a tiny bit of coconut oil or avocado oil for fat and a different flavor.
- cherry tomatoes cut in half (Sungold, if you can get 'em), pieces of cucumber, and frozen corn
- avocado chunks: let baby tap a little salt and pepper, or squeeze a lemon, on top

GOOD TO KNOW

Don't worry if baby is a fruit fiend. Just stick to whole fruit. Nature pairs fiber with sugar, so sugar from whole fruit doesn't have the same harmful effect as refined sugar. Look for dried fruit without added sugar. Skip fruit juice—it's missing the fiber.

Boo, Josh & Wolfie (10 months)

Let baby decide how much to eat

Imagine if someone hovered over, prodded, and cheered on your every bite: annoying!

Trust baby's signals. Our job as parents is to put a variety of nutritious foods in front of our kids. We're in charge of what, when, and where they eat. It's our kids' job to decide whether they eat and how much they eat.

The goal here is to trust children's internal regulation of consumption, which naturally varies day to day. If we continually override kids' signals with our own (well-intentioned) desires, forcing kids to eat the amount of food we think they should eat, they learn to ignore their body's signals for being hungry or full. That sets them up for an unhealthy relationship with food.

We ask baby, "All done?" I'm still trying to get my husband to accept baby's "Yes" instead of responding with, "Are you sure? All done? Here, take one more bite."

Sit down and eat with your child, at regular times. Family meals have more variety and more nutritious foods, studies show, than you get from skipping meals and grazing. (Many of us have the unfortunate view that meals are a duty and snacks are for enjoyment.) If kids ask for food in between their meal and snack times, offer them water. Bonus: regular meal and snack times make for easier naps, as the body gets used to the rhythm of the day.

With new foods, focus on exposure. Encourage baby to touch and smell a new food, watch you eat it, and perhaps put it in her mouth before taking it out again. Think of this not as baby rejecting the food, but as baby preparing to eventually eat the food.

Introduce a new food many more times than you'd think. Children are often skeptical of new foods, and our expectations are way off about how long it takes for them to acclimate. Exposing kids to a new food eight times over two weeks wouldn't be too much. Keep offering variety, but also make sure baby has a familiar food to fill up on.

Don't plead or command over and over. "Take a bite. Just one bite. Come on, eat your food." Studies show that a high rate of verbal pressure leads kids to refuse food.

Bargain sparingly. Rewards and bargaining do work to jump-start exposure to new food, but they're not the best long-term strategy. In one study, researchers asked children to taste slices of red pepper. They told one group, "You can eat as much as you like." They told a second group, "If you eat at least one piece, you may choose one of these stickers. You can eat as much as you like." The reward group jumped to try the red pepper. But over time, children in the first group ate more red pepper and liked it more.

> **TRY THIS**

Now that our toddler is copying everything we do, putting food on our plate instead of her plate is a surefire way to interest her in it.

Baby likes to see us eat the food. Sometimes we play "One bite for mommy, one bite for daddy, one bite for baby."

Offer the opportunity to potty

There's no evidence that later is better than earlier when it comes to potty training. Only that being gentle is better than shaming or forcing baby.

Before World War II, parents often forced, scolded, and punished 8-month-olds into using the toilet. This was linked to problems: constipation, holding it, refusing to use the toilet. Pediatrician T. Berry Brazelton championed an effort to change that practice. That's a good thing. But some parents have interpreted it to mean they should tiptoe around potty training until the child tells you she's done with diapers—a period that's getting longer and longer as diaper companies make bigger and bigger diapers. There's no need to wait *that* long.

No matter what age you choose to help baby use a toilet, here are a few ways to be gentle:

Provide the opportunity only. Rather than physically forcing or bribing baby to sit on the potty, see it as simply offering the opportunity. Baby decides whether to go. You still have to make an effort to encourage baby to sit on the potty and stay sitting, but don't get worked up if she doesn't.

My husband and I sit nearby and sing a song, read a book, or blow bubbles to help baby sit long enough. We remind her, "Yeah, it takes a while to poop. We sit, lean forward, and wait." If she starts to run off, we say, "All done with potty?" rather than "No, no, you're not done. Sit back down."

Offer the potty regularly: before and after sleep, before and after outings, and thirty to sixty minutes after meals. Kids come to expect potty times without being nagged.

"Time for potty" is our line. (Asking our toddler, at 22 months old, "Do you need to go potty?" elicits a "No," even if she's standing there in a half crouch.) As we walk in the door from an outing, we remind her of the routine: "What's the first thing we do when we come home? Sit on the potty." We might add, "Do you need help?" or "What song should we sing?"

Stay low-key. When baby says, "I need to go potty," if we casually respond, "OK, go for it," she will. If we hover or give too much instruction, she'll change her mind. Afterward, if we say, "Good job going potty," she smiles in satisfaction. If we make a big deal, clapping and exclaiming, then the next time she pees, she'll empty her potty in the toilet, then bring it over to us for praise. (Yikes!)

Go diaper-free. My favorite description of potty training is: "You just take off the diaper." You can go diaper-free at pretty much any age, for any amount of time during the day. As early as a few months old, some parents whisk a jar or tiny pot under baby's bum—or hold baby in a squat position over the toilet—between diaper changes. Other parents sit baby on a potty chair when they use the bathroom. Others try to catch every pee and poo, offering a potty every thirty or sixty minutes. Yes, that's how often many infants need to pee. If baby goes, the parents make a noise: "tsss" or "unh, unh." The cue eventually signals baby to go potty, and it gives baby a way to tell you that she needs to go.

We went diaper-free, at home only, around 12 months old. This was hit and miss—meaning, carpet cleaner came in handy. As soon as baby started running to her potty chair on her own, I just expected that she would every time. But she'd get distracted while playing. So would I. In hindsight, I could have more consistently offered her the potty, plus gotten her sitters on the same page.

Save bedtime for last. Most kids wear a diaper to bed at night until age 4 or 5. Medically, the term "bed-wetting" doesn't even apply to kids younger than 5.

GOOD TO KNOW

Potty training doesn't require complete bladder and bowel control, only an ability to briefly delay the action. Indeed, only 20 percent of children have complete bladder and bowel control by age 2, when many parents start potty training.

If you're waiting to potty train, don't put it off past 32 months. Baby might be at higher risk of urinary tract infections, from not completely emptying the bladder. There's also a higher risk of weak bladder control, which leads to more accidents.

Play

Kids learn an incredibly important skill from playing with their peers: self-control. Before that, though, you're baby's favorite toy: baby loves pulling your hair, pinching your nose, stepping up the front of your body, and going for a ride.

Wheeler (5) & Zach (4½)

Let baby touch that

It's hard to beat having a variety of direct, hands-on experiences.

You don't have to buy a mountain of stuff to introduce baby to new stimuli:

- While you're cooking or grocery shopping, let baby touch the papery onion skin and the rough avocado peel.
- In your closet, introduce baby to the cashmere sweater and leather pants you never wear anymore.
- On a walk, when you stop to smell the roses, brush a petal against baby's skin. (Wait until baby is 8 months old, when very light touch feels OK.)
- On our walks, my toddler wants to play hide-and-seek by peeking through the slots of Dumpsters. She wants to touch recycling bins. I've come to terms with this. We can always wash hands afterward.
- Store most of baby's toys and regularly rotate them out.
- Trade toys with friends.

Mmm, rocks

Sensitivity to touch develops in the body from top to bottom, starting with the mouth. That's why babies use their mouths to explore objects. (Rocks were particularly compelling for mine.) If a 1-month-old baby is allowed to mouth an object, but not see it, that baby later can recognize the object visually.

Touch sensitivity takes time to spread down the body: the face is more sensitive than the hands even at age 5.

Tracy & Geneva (23 months)

Save the box

Which toys are best for baby's brain?
Toys that require baby to *use* his brain.

The best toys don't beep, talk, dance, or flash to hold a child's attention. They require imagination to come alive.

But toy manufacturers know that if they say their products boost baby's development—claims that are rarely scientifically tested—you're more likely to buy them. For example, I was given some soft fabric rattles that fasten around baby's wrist. The package says they develop "sound location skills." Really?

Instead, go for basic toys, like these:

- jars with screw-on lids, bowls and cups of various sizes, and something baby can move from one cup to the other (water, dirt, dried beans)
- couch cushions and pillows, set up as an obstacle course for crawling or climbing
- balls and blocks (Lego Duplo, K'Nex sets, Tegu magnetic blocks, Keva Contraptions, Tinkertoys)
- old-fashioned dolls, finger puppets
- chairs and a blanket, for making a fort
- appliance box and markers, for making a car or spaceship
- tape

Don't forget, *you're* baby's favorite toy. Baby loves to climb on you, be twirled, swung, and tossed by you, squeal at the tickle monster—and sit on the floor with you, playing with these toys together.

> **MONEY-SAVING TIP**
>
> Baby's favorite toys are whichever things you didn't buy for baby:
>
> - remote control
> - keys, wallet, cell phone
> - pocket mirror
> - calculator
> - your shoes: putting their feet in them
> - your underwear: wearing it around their neck
> - the box the toy came in
> - fruit: taking one bite of each and putting it back in the bowl
> - laundry basket: going for a spin
> - drawers and cabinets: perfect for hiding your keys, wallet, cell phone

GOOD TO KNOW

Playing with blocks improves spatial skills, math skills, problem-solving skills, and cooperation. Playing with dolls helps baby practice social and emotional skills.

Ross & Naomi (14 months)

Make music with baby

Children encourage you to publicly embarrass
yourself in all sorts of ways you didn't imagine.

My baby and I were out for a walk along a wooded path, and a song popped into my head. As I helped baby touch various parts of the nearest tree, I sang, "And on that twig / there was a leaf / the prettiest leaf / that you ever did see!" Thank you, Toddler Radio on Pandora.

I can barely carry a tune. Good thing infants prefer their parents' voices over other voices, and prefer singing directed to them over other kinds of singing.

We sing at home, too, as I pick out "Twinkle, Twinkle, Little Star" on my baby's xylophone. (Hey, three years of piano lessons didn't go to waste after all!)

And we take a parent-tot music class, because baby gets a taste of music as the social experience that it has been for all of human history. She gets to try out instruments we don't have at home. She dances, bounces, picks up rhythm, and tries out tones. And the teacher is so engaging, my baby gives her a hug at the end of class.

Will music lessons make baby smarter?

Musicians are brainier than non-musicians in all sorts of ways. They're better at abstract reasoning, math, reading, vocabulary, fine motor skills, spatial skills, and working memory.

However, researchers haven't been able to prove that music training is the cause. Perhaps parents who are able to afford private music lessons also read more to their kids, for example, and that's what improves their kids' vocabulary and reading skills. Perhaps children with certain cognitive strengths are attracted to music lessons. The half-dozen trials that have sought to establish a cause report mixed results.

But a brain boost was never the best reason to study music anyway.

≫

Music for music's sake

Music is universal: nearly everyone is drawn to it. "Human societies with no music, like human societies with no language, have never been found," Harvard psychologist Roger Brown wrote. Yet no one has to make a case for studying language—the sounds we use to express what's on our minds versus what's in our souls.

In a piece titled "Why teach music?" Kathryn B. Hull, a nationally certified music teacher, wrote of the many aspects of music:

Music is science. It is "exact and specific." A conductor's score is "a graph which indicates frequencies, intensities, volume changes, melody, and harmony all at once and with precise control of time."

Music is mathematical. It's rhythmically based on fractions of time, "often in multiple combinations simultaneously."

Music is a foreign language. "Most of the terms are in Italian, German, or French; and the notation . . . uses symbols to represent ideas. The semantics of music is the most complete and universal language. It speaks to the soul."

Music is history. It "reflects the environment and times of its creation" and "keeps a people's culture alive."

Music is physical education. "It requires fantastic coordination of fingers, hands, arms, feet, lips, cheeks," along with extraordinary muscle control.

Music is art. What we create and derive from it is "humanism, emotion, feeling— call it what you will."

Hull goes on:

This is why we teach music!

Not because we expect you to major in music
Not because we expect you to play or sing music all your life
Not only so you can relax and just have fun

But

. . . so you will be human
. . . so you will recognize beauty
. . . so you will be sensitive
. . . so you will be closer to an infinite beyond this world
. . . so you will have something to retain for enrichment
. . . so you will have more love, more compassion, more gentleness . . .
in short, more life!

Of what value will it be to make a prosperous living unless you know how to live? Music gives lifelong benefits.

That is why we teach music!

DO IT NOW

Keep a variety of musical instruments in baby's toy bin, and jam together. Libraries and children's museums often offer a free weekly music class. Your local symphony may have a children's program, too. The national research-based programs Music Together and Kindermusik both send you home from class with a CD of the songs you learn.

GOOD TO KNOW

When you listen to music, the brain uses many networks to process rhythm, timbre, and tone. Not only the brain's auditory areas light up, but so do those areas responsible for motor skills, emotions, and creativity.

When playmates grab toys:

Do nothing. *Kids usually figure it out on their own, if you don't step in and make an enormous deal about the toy. It's good practice for them. Agree on this with the other playdate parents ahead of time.*

Make a direct request. *"Your friend would like to play with the toy now. Can you hand it to her? Thank you for sharing!" "Your friend is playing with the toy now. Please wait your turn. Good job waiting." "Your friend is playing with the toy now. You can ask for the toy by saying 'please,' but if she doesn't want to give it to you, you'll need to wait."*

If one child gets upset, empathize and distract. *"You took your friend's toy, and that makes him sad. Can you give your friend a toy?" "Your friend took your toy, and that makes you sad. He'll take a turn, and then you can have a turn. Ooh, a red fire truck! See how the ladder goes up and down?"*

Zach (4 ½) & Wheeler (5)

When kids snatch toys, wait and see

At 18 months old, my toddler and her playmates readily grabbed toys from each other.

Parents almost always stepped in, prying their baby's fingers from the toy, handing it back, and scolding: "She was playing with that." When baby's face crumples in tears, they implore, "We need to share. Can you share?"

Well, no.

In one experiment, children could choose to give food to a partner or not, but would get food either way. At 25 months old, 57 percent decided to share. At 18 months old, only 14 percent decided to share, even though it came at no cost to them.

We want our kids to be able to play nicely with others. But children are capable of altruistic helping only after they've climbed a couple other rungs in this particular developmental ladder.

Cooperation starts early

Notice, though, how cooperative and helpful your toddler is. She tries to feed her favorite food to her playmate. She insists on helping you sweep the floor. We don't have to teach these things. Humans are wired for cooperation (along with competition), say evolutionary anthropologists; it's how our species survived.

It's just that toddlers aren't good at detecting *when* help is needed. That requires an ability to guess someone else's feelings and state of mind. So toddlers understand certain types of help before others.

Instrumental helping: Between 12 and 14 months old, baby begins to help with simple action-based goals, such as looking for or reaching for an item. Around 18 months old, baby's instrumental helping expands to include overcoming obstacles, using tools, and understanding the means to an end.

Empathic helping: Also around 18 months old, baby begins to express concern for and comfort others. Still, emotion-based helping is pretty limited.

By 30 months old, baby is more skilled. Baby can infer others' feelings and intentions, without being told explicitly, and sometimes infer someone's needs.

Altruistic helping: Around 30 months old, baby knows what another person needs, but has trouble giving up something of value. As children gain a greater understanding of the sacrifice that altruism requires, around age 3, they are temporarily even *less* willing to share their possessions.

Help me help you

How much information does a child need to figure out that someone needs help? In one study, led by Margarita Svetlova at the University of Pittsburgh, an adult pretended to be cold. A blanket was within reach of the child but not the adult. The adult went through progressively more explicit cues, five to seven seconds each, until the child brought over the blanket.

1. Gestures: Shivering, rubbing and hugging oneself, saying "Brrr."
2. Naming the internal state: "I'm cold."
3. Stating a general need for an object: "I need something to make me warm."
4. Labeling the object needed: "A blanket!"
5. Nonverbal request: Looking at the child, then the blanket, then the child.
6. Less subtle nonverbal request: Gesturing to the blanket.
7. General verbal request: "Can you help me?"
8. Specific verbal request: "Can you bring me the blanket?"

Guess at which point the average 18-month-old figured it out. Step 6. But by 30 months? Step 2. Unless it was the child's own blanket that the child had to share. Then, the 30-month-old resisted until Step 4. So, it's not that an 18-month-old can't help, cooperate, or share. He just needs explicit instructions about someone else's state of mind. Your toddler's peers are unlikely to offer these kinds of instruction—but you can.

Play at self-control

Self-control is one of the most important skills your child can develop.

As you can imagine, the ability to start or continue doing something you'd rather not do (like your homework), and the ability to stop doing something you want to do (like watching TV), is a powerful force in creating a successful life.

Many, many studies show this to be the case. Leading researcher Adele Diamond summarizes a landmark 2011 study by Terrie Moffitt, who followed a thousand children for thirty-two years:

> Children with worse self-control (less persistence, more impulsivity, and poorer attention regulation) at ages 3–11 tend to have worse health, earn less, and commit more crimes 30 years later than those with better self-control as children, controlling for IQ, gender, social class, and more.

Self-control—also called self-regulation or inhibitory control—is core to a suite of brain processes called executive function. Inhibitory control, working memory, attention, and cognitive flexibility combine to allow problem solving, reasoning, planning, and delaying gratification.

As students, children with more self-control are

- better able to focus on and complete their assignments,
- better able to pay attention and ignore distractions, and
- better able to integrate new material.

Executive function starts to develop during baby's first year of life. But it won't fully mature until your baby is in his or her early 20s. That's a lot of time to practice.

There are plenty of engaging ways to put the "fun" in executive function:

Tell your own stories

Kids love storytelling. You're looking at each other instead of at a book, getting that face-to-face interaction. And the lack of pictures exercises children's ability to pay attention and keep track of details. Children remember more of the characters and plot from storytelling than from book reading, studies show.

If you're not comfortable telling stories, you could start by recounting your day to your infant, and expand your repertoire from there. Baby doesn't care what the story is about! My stories tend to start with "There once was a girl . . . " and involve whatever exotic thing happened yesterday. You can also look for storytelling events at festivals, schools, and bookstores.

Dance, kick, and make music

See if your child enjoys traditional martial arts, dance, or playing a musical instrument—especially with others. All of these require your child to concentrate, pay attention for long stretches, and hold in mind complex sequences: the steps of the dance, the notes of the song.

Diamond says they also provide joy, give a sense of social belonging, develop motor skills, instill pride, and promote self-confidence—all of which support executive-function development.

≫

OTHER WAYS TO BUILD EXECUTIVE FUNCTION

Exercise. This is one of the best ways to build executive function, among other things (see page 12). Less obviously, yoga and Tae Kwon Do (if noncompetitive) also have been shown to improve executive function in kids.

Set challenging goals: At age 3, building a taller block tower, for example; at age 5, building a birdhouse.

Hobbies: Encourage a passion that takes your child's active effort.

Montessori school: Kids in this program tend to have higher levels of executive function and creativity.

Allow mistakes: See page 147.

A second language: See page 65.

Make-believe: See page 115.

Quentin (2) & Sonia

Play games

Classic kids' games are great, too. I remember playing several of these as a kid with my parents and sisters. Not only are they a blast, they help build executive function. In one study, preschoolers played such games for thirty minutes twice a week. After eight weeks, the children's self-regulation scores were significantly better, compared with those in the control group. The researchers, led by Megan McClelland at Oregon State University, studied 276 low-income preschoolers.

The key is that the activity becomes progressively more challenging (with games, you might increase the speed, add rules, or reverse the rules) as kids get the hang of it. Music and movement help, too, so kids don't have to sit still for long.

Here are the traits to look for in games that develop executive function:

Games that require inhibiting one's natural reaction

Freeze: Create a playlist that alternates between your favorite slow and fast songs. Everybody dances when you play the music, and everybody freezes when you hit stop. Dance slowly to slow songs and quickly to fast songs—then the opposite.

Color-Matching Freeze: Tape various colors of construction paper to the ground. Follow the rules above, except also hold up a color when the music stops. Everybody has to run and stand on that color paper before freezing.

Conducting an Orchestra: When one person is "conducting," the others play their instruments (bells or pots and pans or whatever you have). When the conductor puts down the baton, the playing stops. Then switch the rule so that the players play quickly when the baton waves quickly, and vice versa. Try opposites: when one person is conducting, the others stop playing, and vice versa.

Games that require paying close attention

Drumbeats: Come up with body movements (like clapping, stomping, walking, or dancing). Match them to drum cues. Kids could walk quickly to fast drumming, walk slowly to slow drumming, and freeze when you stop drumming. Or they could hop to fast drumbeats and crawl to slow drumbeats.

Walk in a Line: Make a game of walking along a line in the sidewalk, the line between planks in a wooden floor, painters' tape you've put across the carpet, or a log on the ground.

Games that require cognitive flexibility

Sleeping, Sleeping, All the Children Are Sleeping: The kids pretend to sleep while you sing, "Sleeping, sleeping, all the children are sleeping." Then make up an animal that the kids have to stand up and act out, saying: "And when they woke up . . . they were monkeys!"

Games that require focusing on one thing while ignoring others

Slug Bug: When kids see a Volkswagen Beetle during a drive, they yell "Slug bug!" Or "Yellow car!" or whatever color/car model/phrase you come up with. They can rack up points instead of punches if you prefer.

Alphabet: Find each letter of the alphabet, in order, on signs and buildings (and, for a faster game, license plates) during a drive.

Games that work on working memory

Clap Your Hands: Cut a big square, circle, and triangle from construction paper. Have one person choose an action for each shape, such as clap your hands (square); stomp your feet (circle); and touch your nose (triangle). The leader holds up or points to the shapes in order (square, circle, triangle, repeat), performing each action to demonstrate. Then the leader indicates the shapes in order as the kids perform the matching action together. Try going faster and faster. Try switching cues so that the kids must also inhibit what they just learned: touch your toes (square); raise your arms (circle); jump (triangle). The leader continues indicating the shapes in order.

I'm Going on Vacation and I'm Bringing . . . The first player lists an item that starts with A. The second player repeats that item and adds one that starts with B. The next player repeats both items and adds one that starts with C, etc.

What executive functions look like

	Child	Adult
Inhibitory control *ability to resist the urge to do one thing and instead do what is most appropriate*	• resists a smaller reward if given the option of a greater reward in the future • goes to the end of the line instead of cutting • reaches around a glass display instead of trying to reach straight for an item inside	• stops binge-watching *Breaking Bad*, turning off the TV instead of hitting "Next episode" • thinks before speaking • goes for the fruit instead of the cake after resolving to eat more fruit and less cake
Working memory *ability to hold information in mind and work with it*	• connects a phrase from a song to something seen during a walk • does a math problem in her head	• relates something read in a history book to a current political event • mentally reorders errands based on their distance from the house
Attention *ability to focus your attention and resist distraction*	• concentrates on building a castle, despite a sibling racing around • looks for mom in the mall, screening out everything else to see only her face	• resists posting on social media to complete a project for work • at a party, concentrates on the conversation at hand, even though many people are speaking
Cognitive flexibility *ability to switch perspectives; ability to adjust to changed demands or priorities*	• changes strategies when action isn't getting the desired result • during make-believe, goes with the flow as characters change	• sees different peoples' points of view, or sees their reasons for saying what they said or wanting what they wanted • finds an alternate route when the planned route is blocked • adjusts when things don't go according to plan

THE RESEARCH

Many studies show that preschoolers' and kindergarteners' executive-function scores are more important than their IQ scores for later academic success. Young children with better executive function

- tend to be more than three months ahead of their peers in early literacy,
- have higher levels of academic achievement from elementary school through college,
- do better on standardized tests, such as the SAT,

- tend to have positive relationships with peers and teachers (they're less disruptive, inconsiderate, or aggressive, which in turn boosts their academic achievement), and
- are more likely to finish college.

Henry (3) & Hope

What makes a great playroom

It doesn't matter how big your play space is or where you put it (ours seems to be the middle of the living room). What matters is that you create opportunities for a variety of experiences.

Think art, science, and imaginative play: Instruments for making music. Clothes for dress-up. Supplies for drawing and creating props. A microscope, a calculator, and kits for science. Newspapers and magazines. Blocks and more blocks, cardboard boxes and tubes, dolls and cups.

Encourage your child's interests, however random. If your child becomes obsessed with something (garbage trucks, fairies, dinosaurs), riff on the theme.

As often as you can, get into that other wonderful playroom: the great outdoors.

Paige (5)

Make-believe

One particular type of play is beneficial to your child's brain. It's play in which children become fully engrossed in pretending to be someone else.

Kids spiritedly discuss who they're going to be and what they're going to do.

"OK, we're going to play house. I'm going to be the mom."

"I want to be the mom!"

"No, I'm the mom and you're the baby, and I'm going to feed you lunch."

"OK, then we take the dog for a walk."

And then they act it out.

It's called mature make-believe play—a serious-sounding name for something so fun. Maybe that's because this type of play is actually quite structured. It requires following the rules of what it means to be a mom or baby, and the steps required to make a meal or walk a dog. If a kid starts wandering outside those rules, the other kids bring him back in line.

What this does for the brain is build executive function: the skill set that allows children to set goals, plan, stay on task, and avoid distraction (see page 106).

THE RESEARCH

In an early-education program called Tools of the Mind, students spend the majority of their time on activities that build executive function—mainly play. In a study of 150 kids, the children in Tools of the Mind classrooms scored 30 percent to nearly 100 percent better on executive-function tests than kids in the control group. They also were

- more creative (asked to think of various uses for specific objects, they came up with three times more ideas),
- more facile with language,
- better at problem solving,
- half as stressed, and
- more socially skilled.

Model how to make-believe

Age 1 to 3: Model pretending

Children are just beginning to learn to play with objects in a pretend way.

Teach your child how to pretend. Take an empty cup and pretend to drink from it. Say, "Let's pretend to make dinner," as you stir a spoon in a pot and then pretend to taste it. Then say, "Now *you* make dinner," and follow what the child does.

Make up a role. "Let's pretend we're ____ (Dad, Grandma, Auntie, Uncle) making dinner." Model what that person would say. "Grandma would say, 'Do you want cookies for dinner?'" Try to use speech that the child has heard before. Ideally, children will act and sound like the person they are playing.

Set up a play space that is defined, consistent, and accessible. Don't be too quick to put things away.

Have props around, like old clothes and shoes, purses and briefcases, pretend doctors' kits and carpenter tools.

Include blocks and household objects, like cups and spoons, that can become other things with some imagination.

Avoid toys that "do the thinking" for the child. Choose toys that are an easy size for children to manipulate, such as baby dolls that a child can dress and undress, hold, and bathe.

Age 3 to 5: Help with ideas, act out a role

Children have an idea of how to pretend but need ideas of what to pretend.

Use everyday chores, errands, and situations to set up play ideas. Point out people, and talk about what they say and do. Your child can pretend to be them when you get home.

Act out a story your child likes.

Make up props. Don't buy a doctor's uniform— instead, use a grown-up's old shirt and make a stethoscope out of string with a circle attached to it. Creating something symbolic takes more thought.

Take a secondary role. You want your child to direct the play scene as much as possible, telling you what to do and what will come next. For example, your child could be the doctor and you could be the patient or the father of a sick baby.

Help your child expand the roles and add to the script. "Now, what could happen next? Can we pretend that we had to go to the hospital in an ambulance? What else could happen?"

After playing a role and a scene several times, suggest a new twist. What if you were the doctor on a pirate ship? In outer space? Have the same role happen in a different place.

Introduce simple games with rules. Board games like Chutes and Ladders and Candy Land are an extension of make-believe play.

Age 5 and up: Kids play on their own

Children can act out elaborate scenes by themselves or with other children, using props they created.

You become more of a resource, providing ideas to help get things going, rather than being a part of the play.

Have props available and materials (blocks, pieces of fabric, blankets, paper, scissors, glue) that children can use to make their own props.

Children will begin to play more with little dolls and action figures instead of dressing up and playing the roles themselves. They may engage in "director's play," in which they talk and act for the figures, playing several roles and changing their voices for each of the actors.

Use stories and literature as a basis for play. Encourage children to make their own versions of familiar stories or to make completely new stories, and then act them out.

Play board and card games with simple rules.

If you have more than one child, help the older child teach the younger sibling what to do and say.

Phoebe (2 ½) & Jenn

Nurture creativity

What will life look like twenty-some years from now, when your baby has grown up?

It's almost impossible to imagine. Our world is so unpredictable that navigating it smartly will require some ingenuity on the part of your children. Creativity will be an important skill for a citizen of this future. Whether your children become entrepreneurs, artists, tradespeople or academics, or work for private enterprises, governments or nonprofits, the world that hires them will be looking for creative thinkers.

Historically, people have used IQ tests to predict a child's success in school and in life beyond. IQ tests give a useful measure of linguistic, logical (mathematical), and spatial abilities. But researchers, entrepreneurs, and educators increasingly agree that creativity—something IQ tests don't measure—is just as valuable in our rapidly changing society.

Can creativity be measured? It can. The Torrance Tests of Creative Thinking have been used for decades by schools to assess students' abilities to create ideas that are original, diverse, and elaborate. One exercise might give a curved line with the instruction "Finish this drawing," for example.

Ways to practice creativity

Creative-thinking ability is one-third genetics and two-thirds practice, according to studies of twins separated at birth. Here are ideas for developing creative skills in your child:

- Encourage your child to turn an interest into a passion.
- Allow and encourage mistakes. "If you're not prepared to be wrong, you'll never come up with anything original," notes creativity expert Sir Ken Robinson.

- Sign your child up for visual arts, drama, or reading programs.
- Recognize your child's talents and support them.
- Show more interest in what your children have learned than in their grades.
- Encourage your children to come up with multiple potential solutions for a problem.
- Rather than giving the answers, give your child the tools to find the answers.
- Model the concept of thinking visually: when you have a spatial dilemma, like how to rearrange your furniture, sketch it out with your child.
- Use analogies and metaphors to stimulate new ways of thinking.

Compiled from published interviews with Paul Torrance and Sir Ken Robinson

TRY THIS

How might you help your child turn an interest into a passion? Go all in. If he's drawn to maps, you could plaster his room with maps, play geography games, make a 3-D map of your street out of playdough, hunt for unusual maps at antique shops, use tracing paper to create maps, go geocaching, help him photocopy your city map and chart the route for the day's outings, look at various representations of one location (aerial photos, maps showing topography, climate, or resources), brainstorm how he'd change a map if he were a city planner, take him to visit a cartographer . . .

DO IT NOW When you see a scene during a walk, make a game of guessing what's happening, what caused it, and what might happen next.

Ask "Why?" and "What if?"

No one asks more questions than 4-year-olds. And then they go to school.

Children "quickly learn that teachers value the right answers more than provocative questions," says researcher Hal Gregersen in *Harvard Business Review*. "And by the time they're grown up and are in corporate settings, they have already had the curiosity drummed out of them."

How can you create an environment where your child can keep asking "Why?" and "Why not?" and "What if?"

Be a tour guide
Constantly describing and explaining the world around you is one way. I like this story from a stay-at-home dad (who also happens to be a personal-finance blogger):

I usually spend about six hours a day just playing and learning with my son. I view myself as one of those automated tour guide devices that you can walk around with in a museum—except I'm available to him wherever we are in life.

"Why did the water in the creek flood this dam we made yesterday, Dada?"

"Well, did you notice how it's hot outside today? Look at the thermometer on my watch—86 degrees Fahrenheit, or 30 Celsius. Now look up into the mountains where this creek is coming from. What do you think is happening to the snow on a hot day like today?"

Excerpted with permission from "Avoiding Ivy League Preschool Syndrome," mrmoneymustache.com

I try to do the same with my toddler. She loves talking about bicycles, putting on helmets, and spinning the pedals of bikes we pass on the sidewalk. So when my bike tire got a flat, I let her squeeze each tire to feel the difference, help me pull off the tire, and push the air pump. It was more interesting for both of us than shooing her away from the dirty job.

Another day, when she kept getting into some tea candles on a closet shelf, I took one into a dark room. She sat in my lap as I lit it. We talked quietly about how beautiful fire is, and how a flame is hot if you touch it. She held a tiny finger over the flame before pulling away: a baby's version of playing with fire.

Why not?

IS IT HARD TO THINK DIFFERENTLY?

Not for a 4-year-old. But more than 60 percent of adults in a Harvard study said that it's uncomfortable or exhausting to think differently. However, if adults repeatedly practice, they report that it becomes energizing.

Connect

Mini manifesto: Let's spend more time on the floor with our kids. Let's trade strollers for newborn carriers, and car trips for walks. Let's spend more time looking into each other's eyes, and less time staring into our screens. Let's really get to know each other.

Percy & Amelia (4)

Ask for help

"I feel like I should be able to handle it."

That's what my neighbor said in explaining why she hadn't taken me up on my offer to babysit. "No, it's OK," another friend said as she juggled both kids into the restaurant bathroom instead of leaving me to entertain one kid in her high chair.

It's hard to ask for help. We don't want to burden anyone, or we think needing help is a failure on our part, that we're supposed to be able to handle this parenting thing by ourselves.

If something is keeping you from asking for help, please get over it.

Imagine if a friend asked *you* for help. You would be more than happy to oblige (unless your baby is 0 to 6 months old, in which case you're still in shock).

But we have collectively forgotten that it is impossible to raise another human without help. It's not an issue of whether you're mentally tough enough to do it. Our species did not evolve to raise children solo, and only relatively recently has it become a typical experience. Over and over, I've seen unrealistic self-expectations lead to isolation, depression, desperation, or guilt.

 **DO IT NOW** Ask!

Many hands make light work

I didn't truly understand what "It takes a village to raise a child" means until I found myself in a two-bedroom hotel suite on a weekend away with my toddler, mom, two sisters, 14-year-old niece, and 9-year-old nephew. As we reconnected over hair talk, impromptu makeovers, and family stories, my baby ran around the suite. Whoever was nearby watched her. What a difference! The burden wasn't too great on any one of us. It felt fantastic. And I felt that sense of relief even though I have an incredibly helpful husband, ten hours a week of babysitting, dear friends, and a lot of patience.

If you haven't spent much time around babies before you had your own (I hadn't), your idea of how much work a baby takes may be waaaay off. In one tribal culture, it's not uncommon for *fourteen* people to watch a baby in an eight-hour span. So build more of a support network than you think you need.

Unless your parents or siblings are planning to move in next door, you'll need to build a community through friends and neighbors. (See page 8 for ideas.) Once you've done that, actually use it.

My neighbor and I agreed that she would have accepted my offer to babysit if I had more aggressively inserted myself, as in: "I'm free to borrow your baby on Thursday. What time is good for you?" So that's what I said the next time I offered—and she said, "Noon."

Abyaz, Melinda, Parveen & Alianna (5 days)

Choose empathy first

Here's one of the best things you can do for your marriage: in an emotional situation, make empathy your first response.

We often jump to offer advice, play devil's advocate, defend the person upsetting our partner, or change the subject. All our partner really wants is empathy: for us to identify with what they're feeling. So truly listen. Show that you understand how your partner feels.

"I'm sorry. I hate it when that happens. I can understand how that would be frustrating."

"Oh, baby, that is so disappointing. I know you had your heart set on that."

"I hear you. That never feels good."

What empathy does
Empathy literally calms the body. The brain uses the vagus nerve to monitor and control the state of your organs. When your brain senses empathy, it signals the vagus nerve to relax your body by slowing your heart rate or lowering your blood pressure.

Why empathy is key to relationships
Empathy is powerful in a marriage because a resolution doesn't exist for the majority of disagreements. The people involved simply have differing values, motivations, or desires. Your best path through the conflict is to simply show understanding.

One of the perpetual conflicts my husband and I have is that I'm a night owl and he's an early riser. If I stayed up too late, my husband used to lecture me about personal responsibility. But he's more empathetic these days.

"Did you sleep OK?" he asked.

"No, maybe four hours," I said. "I stayed up too late."

"I'm sorry," he said. "What can I do to help?"

The first time I got that kind of response, relief and gratitude flowed through me. I felt supported instead of attacked. I felt closer to my husband instead of at odds with him. That's kind of amazing for eight little words.

TRY THIS

Choosing empathy first with our newborn, too, was a big help. Considering baby's perspective (as often as we could) kept us from growing irritated over spending yet another hour bouncing baby, or changing yet another diaper in the middle of the night. My husband was good at this. "I'm sorry you're sad," he would tell our crying newborn. "It must be hard to be a baby." Or "Let's change your diaper. I know I always feel better with a clean diaper." That always made me laugh.

Empathy works well as baby gets older, too. If your child wants something he can't have, for example, try saying, "Yes, that would be so nice, wouldn't it? We can't do that right now, because of X, but we can do this other thing."

Or "Yes, you would like more blueberries. I know, that would taste so good! You just ate a lot, so we're going to wait until later to have more." Or "Those are scissors. You would like to play with them. They're sharp, and they could hurt you, so I'm going to put them away. But we can draw instead."

Baby feels heard, and your conversation is saved from being a frustrating series of "No, don't touch that," "No, don't do that," and "No, you can't have that."

Create more ups than downs

Every marriage has conflicts.

It doesn't matter whether the two of you tend to calmly compromise, have big blow-ups and then make up, or rarely confront your differences. All three styles of dealing with inevitable conflicts can make for happy, stable relationships.

The important thing, marriage researcher John Gottman says, is that your marriage has more positive interactions (touching, smiling, complimenting, etc.) than negative ones. In happy marriages, it's a five-to-one ratio. Not that you're keeping track, exactly.

Summarizing thirty-five years of research, Gottman says happily married couples

- behave like good friends,
- handle their conflicts in gentle and positive ways,
- repair negative interactions during an argument, and
- fully process negative emotions.

On the flip side, Gottman found four corrosive behaviors that, if couples engage in them regularly, lead to divorce in an average of five and a half years:

Criticism: stating your complaints as a personality defect in your partner. For example: "You always leave messes lying around for me to clean up. Why do you have to be so lazy?" rather than, "I would appreciate it if we could do the dishes together."

Contempt: making statements from a position of superiority, often while thinking that the other person is a total moron ("*That's* not the right way to do it").

Defensiveness: denying responsibility ("I wouldn't have . . . if you hadn't . . ."), blaming circumstances beyond your control, or immediately responding with a complaint of your own ("You're not perfect, either"), rather than acknowledging your partner's complaint.

Stonewalling: instead of giving the usual signals that you're listening (nodding, "mm-hmm," "go on"), you sit in stony silence.

> "*Rather than becoming defensive and hurtful, [masters of marriage] pepper their disputes with flashes of affection, intense interest, and mutual respect.*"
>
> **John Gottman, The Relationship Cure**

It's how you handle your conflicts—not a lack of conflict—that makes for a good relationship. The same thing is true of your relationship with your kids.

THE RESEARCH

John Gottman, one of the nation's leading marriage and parenting researchers, runs the "Love Lab" at the University of Washington. He has predicted with 94 percent success whether couples will stay together. Gottman has studied more than three thousand couples in researching why some marriages end in divorce and others remain strong.

Know your child

Children all have their own temperaments.

Some babies are calm, cool, and collected. They'll eat everything from beet borscht to coconut quinoa. Raining? Sunny? Great. They want to be outside. If they get upset, it doesn't last. If you explain why they can't have something, they generally accept it. If you show them something, they want to try it.

Other babies are much more sensitive to change. They like to eat the same thing at the same time in the same way. They hang back. They startle and cry at an unfamiliar toy or person. On the flip side, they are fiercely loyal, given time. They're cautious about trying to do new things.

Still other babies run headfirst into whatever interests them—and everything interests them. They have boundless energy; their parents become sprinters, on-the-alert anticipators, and rapid redirectors. They're incredibly persistent, even manipulative. Sensitive to change, their moods are intense.

They were just born this way.

Researchers Stella Chess and Alexander Thomas were the first to categorize temperament. Collecting data on nearly 140 children from 1956 to 1988, Thomas and Chess identified nine dimensions of temperament: activity, regularity, initial reaction, adaptability, intensity, mood, distractibility, persistence/attention span, and sensitivity.

Because of this work, researchers now recognize that babies are born with a temperament, that it is fairly stable throughout childhood, that parents have only limited influence over it, and that it influences one's parenting style, too.

Thomas and Chess found that 65 percent of children fell into the following three categories, and the rest of the children were a combination:

TYPES OF TEMPERMENT

Flexible / Easy 40% of children	Feisty / Spirited / Difficult 10% of children	Cautious / Slow to warm up 15% of children
pretty adaptable	don't adapt easily to change	don't adapt easily to change
regular patterns of eating and sleeping	irregular patterns of eating and sleeping	regular or irregular patterns of eating and sleeping
approach new stimuli with ease	withdraw from new stimuli	withdraw from new stimuli
react mildly to change	react intensely to change	initially react mildly to change, but form an opinion after multiple exposures

TRY THIS

Many of my friends get anxious that I let my baby tackle a climbing wall for bigger kids or let her roam a little farther outdoors. And I get anxious that they don't let their babies do these things. Of course, each of us knows our babies, and we're usually doing the right things for them (and us).

But as new parents, uncertain of our choices, it's easy to feel judged.

Try heading off the disapproval of others by helping them understand your baby. "She takes time to warm up; it's best if you hang back and let her come to you," you might say of a shy baby. Or "Yes, he's a feisty one. We really admire that he puts his whole heart into things."

No one temperament is better than another

Of the nine dimensions Thomas and Chess identified, no one aspect is ideal in all situations. Persistence might help your child make the team, and at the same time wear you down during disagreements. Shyness might protect your child from becoming a troublemaker, and at the same time mean your child misses out on opportunities in school.

While temperament may remain relatively stable, baby's expression of it doesn't. A shy child can learn to become more comfortable socially with gentle guidance, for example. Researcher Jerome Kagan found that children at the extreme ends of the spectrum migrate toward the middle by age 7.

Temperament doesn't predict who your child will become so much as it predicts who your child will not become.

Creating a good fit

What will you think of your baby's temperament? That depends on your own. Any temperament will seem difficult to deal with if it doesn't fit your own values, style, and expectations.

"Goodness of fit," Thomas and Chess called it.

If you and baby aren't naturally a good fit, you can create a better one by adjusting your expectations, your style, and baby's environment (such as finding ways for a rambunctious child to spend more time outdoors). Even if you and baby are a good fit, it takes time to get to know your child and understand how to parent accordingly.

For example, my toddler seemed confident trying new things, so I assumed she would feel immediately comfortable joining a group of new people. I'd plop her in the middle and step to the side. She would come hug my leg. I would be a little disappointed. Soon I figured out that I needed to sit with her or hold her for a minute, and then she'd happily join in.

Temperamental baby

No matter baby's temperament, baby is sometimes going to be temperamental. There's the evening "witching hour," when for some reason newborns get super fussy and nothing you do helps.

There's the sudden appearance of toddlers' insistent "*No!*" to whatever you do ("No, that's *my* leg!" as I put on baby's pants). And as baby's sense of self continues to emerge, there's the stubborn "By self!" or "*I* do it!"—especially when you don't have time for baby to "do it."

Parenting a feisty baby

"Feisty" kids are the most challenging for anyone to parent, as they tend to be irritable and react grandly to small things. Some things you can do to help:

Stay engaged. Over time, studies show, mothers tend to withdraw from highly reactive babies, increasingly ignoring them and playing less with them. Counteract this tendency by approaching each encounter with empathy and an understanding that the most important thing is for baby to feel safe.

Get coaching. In one study, parents of "feisty" 6-month-olds received three months of training in being sensitive to their child's needs. At 12 months old, 70 percent of those infants were deemed securely attached, compared with 30 percent of infants whose parents didn't receive training. You can look for a parenting class or a parent coach, or read *Raising Your Spirited Child* by Mary Sheedy Kurcinka.

Commit to consistency. Parents of highly reactive children tend to become inconsistent in their discipline, which leads to a more highly reactive child.

Defuse conflicts. If both child and mother have highly reactive temperaments, the child is likely to become more, not less, defiant and aggressive. When you get upset, call a time-out (or calm-down) for yourself (see page 172) to avoid escalating conflicts.

Hold weekly family meetings

When are you going to talk about how things are working (or not working) in your family?

While you're all rushing off to school and work? In the middle of a tantrum or argument? During the one meal you eat together, when you'd rather talk about everyone's day?

Try a twenty-minute weekly family meeting instead. According to Bruce Feiler in *The Secrets of Happy Families*, devotees report

- less stress, more communication, and more productivity;
- kids coming up with creative solutions to their own problems; and
- calmer decision making ("I see you're upset about this. Let's put it on our family-meeting agenda").

How it works

Set a day and time, like Sunday evenings, that you promise not to schedule over. The meeting should focus on the family as a unit rather than on individuals. Involve the kids around age 3.

Ask three questions:

1. **What worked well in our family this past week?**
   You could start by having each family member compliment every other family member: "I liked it when . . ." or "I appreciated that . . ."
2. **What went wrong in our family this past week?**
   Keep it civil.
3. **What will we work on this coming week?**
   Choose one or two problems to focus on, and brainstorm solutions together. Don't shoot down any of the ideas right away; that shuts down creative thinking. Get all of the ideas out there, evaluate them as a family, and choose one solution together. Agree to try it out for a certain amount of time, then reevaluate it at a later family meeting.

Allow a few weeks for everyone to practice and get comfortable with the concept. Afterward, some families watch a movie or go for ice cream, so the idea of a weekly meeting is more fun.

Mahmud, Alianna (5 days old), Abyaz, Melinda & Parveen

Put down your phone

I can hear your sputters of protest already:
Is such an *extreme* measure *really* necessary?

Science can't tell you for sure. There is no definitive research (yet) about the effects of smartphones and other digital devices. But we do know a few important things about ourselves as humans, and these things can help inform how and when you use your phone.

We are social animals. We thrive on face-to-face interaction, and we don't function well without it. Human interaction is so important that, in baby's first years, it is what turns on the brain for certain types of learning (see page 65).

The most important thing in your child's life is his or her relationships. With you, with siblings, with friends; eventually with classmates and teachers, with colleagues and bosses, with romantic partners, with his or her own children. What makes for good relationships? Things you learn through lots of face-to-face interaction: communication skills, empathy, and control over your emotions and behavior. A large part of communication is nonverbal: interpreting facial expressions, gestures, and body language.

Children need a ton of practice reading other people. Studies show how much time it takes to understand nonverbal communication:

- Three-year-olds are better than 2-year-olds at understanding the facial expressions that add meaning to an utterance (such as a look implying "you need to do this" with a directive to clean up the toys).
- Four-year-olds are able to identify and communicate emotions in body movement at a rate better than chance; 5-year-olds are even better at it.
- Eight-year-olds are as good at reading nonverbal signs as adults.

Children can't practice reading people if one (or both) of you is buried in a device.

Great relationships are the secret to happiness. Being truly present with your child, partner, and friends makes for more fulfilling relationships. And that's the key to the good life.

PHONE BAN

I have a personal ban on checking my phone or opening up my laptop when baby's around.

I fail at least once a day. But I can see that it's worth trying. I can tell that my digital devices suck me in for longer than I intend. And I can tell that my baby is upset about being ignored—just as I am when I'd like to communicate with someone and they're more entranced by a glowing screen.

So I'll send a quick text message in the kitchen while baby's busy in her high chair. I may check in just before a run, when she's facing away in the jogging stroller. I've turned off the automatic e-mail sync, so I don't see a visual indicator on my phone that I have e-mail, and feel the need to read it right then. My phone is often set to vibrate, so it's not a distraction. My laptop is tucked away until nap time or bedtime.

I'm not saying we should avoid digital devices entirely. But it is worth considering how much of our time they should take up, and how and when they should be used (see page 144).

These days, it takes effort to create conditions that encourage, not discourage, real live interaction.

Wolfie (10 months)

(Almost) no TV before age 2

What's so wrong with a little TV? Most people would say, "Nothing."

That must be why 40 percent of babies are watching TV by 3 months old, and 90 percent of tots are watching one to two hours of TV or videos per day by age 2.

When the American Academy of Pediatrics issued its 1996 policy statement on TV for kids, most media reported AAP's stance as "zero TV before age 2." That's widely seen as unrealistic. In a 2013 update, the AAP "discourages" TV.

Either way, what's the problem with TV for baby? A few things.

- **There are no known positive effects of babies watching TV.** Not even educational videos marketed for infants. The human brain is wired to learn from humans, at least early on. Face-to-face interaction literally acts like a gatekeeper for the brain, determining whether certain kinds of learning will happen—or not.
- **TV hurts language skills.** Babies who watched *Baby Einstein* videos knew fewer vocabulary words than babies who didn't watch. The study results were such a reversal of the product's claims that Disney, who produced the videos, offered refunds to parents. Two studies found that *Sesame Street* hurt expressive language for kids under age 2 (although after age 2 it helped in other areas, such as school readiness).
- **When the TV is on, babies aren't interacting.** Kids don't get face-to-face interaction. They're not hearing you talk. They're not exploring or playing or moving—key activities for development.

Baby isn't interacting . . . um, that's the point, right? TV isn't *for* the baby; it's for the break *from* baby. It gets a toddler to sit still for thirty minutes instead of, for example, emptying all the drawers while you're trying to clean the house. "Educational" videos just make you feel less guilty about it.

Perhaps the real issues are these:

Parents need a break, and we're not asking for the help we need from our partners, neighbors, family, and friends. (See pages 8 and 124 for ideas.)

Parents want to get stuff done. This is so much easier when baby is otherwise occupied. But it's less stressful if we can align our expectations with our new reality. Knowing baby is the priority when you're together avoids the tension created by competing priorities. Sure, we'll get less done. Yes, any task will take five times longer. On the other hand, what's truly wrong with that?

A TINY BIT OF TV

My husband and I have a no-TV policy. Sure, our baby has seen some TV. There was the time a sitter asked if the baby could watch videos on her cell phone, then let it slip: "She loves it!" We've visited folks accustomed to having the TV on during dinner, and we've made exceptions for sports play-off games.

But I like our TV ban. It definitely makes us more aware of when a TV is on. And it's clear that baby gets more (and more interesting) interaction from us when the TV is off. That fits with research showing that when the TV is on, parents' interaction with their kids drops by 20 percent.

I'm also relieved that the AAP's policy isn't a complete ban. One less thing to feel guilty about.

A little TV after age 2

After age 2, kids can learn something valuable from interactive TV shows.

Look for shows where the characters

- speak directly to your child,
- provide opportunities for your child to respond, and
- label objects.

Educational shows with those characteristics, like *Blue's Clues* and *Dora the Explorer*, can improve vocabulary, social skills, and school readiness. Common Sense Media (commonsensemedia.org) has ratings and reviews to help you choose.

What's so magical about age 2? Somewhere between 18 months and 30 months, researchers found, a child's ability to process information changes, and kids are better able to focus attention on TV. With repeated exposure to a screen, kids learn how to extract information from it.

Vocabulary
After watching interactive shows, kids in one study knew more vocabulary words than kids in the control group (and fewer vocabulary words after watching noninteractive shows). See the chart at right.

Social skills
Pop quiz: Should your 3-year-old watch the crude adult cartoon *King of the Hill*? Or Nickelodeon's *Wonder Pets!* show about team players? A recent study shows that you can reduce physical aggression in preschoolers by switching aggressively themed adult shows to children's shows with a pro-social message (showing empathy, helping others, or resolving disputes without violence).

School readiness
Low-income and moderate-income kids who watched educational shows (like *Sesame Street*, *Mister Rogers*, and *3-2-1 Contact*) had higher academic test scores three years later than kids who didn't watch the shows.

WORDS KIDS KNEW AFTER WATCHING SHOWS

TV program	Vocabulary
Blue's Clues, *Dora the Explorer*	13.3 more words
Barney & Friends, *Teletubbies*	10–11.7 fewer words
Disney movies	no more or fewer words

The trouble with two-plus hours a day of TV

Children can learn from a screen, but the American Academy of Pediatrics still recommends less than one or two hours a day of time in front of a TV—or any other screen—for children older than 2. Here's why:

Time spent watching TV predicts obesity. When kids are watching TV, they're eating more and exercising less. Watching TV is so passive that one's metabolic rate drops even lower than when sitting at a desk. More than two hours of TV or videos a day is a health risk.

Kids miss out on reading. In families where the TV is almost always on (and that's 30 percent of families with young kids), reading time gets shafted by 25 percent at ages 3 and 4, and nearly 40 percent at ages 5 and 6, compared to other families.

Background TV distracts kids from play. When the TV is on in the background, kids may not appear to be paying attention to it, glancing at the TV only sporadically. But between ages 1 and 3, the kids play for less time, are less focused during play, skip from one toy to another, and play in a less sophisticated way. (See page 106 for the importance of play.)

Attention spans shorten. Kids who watch more than two hours of TV per day, studies show, appear to have more trouble focusing attention.

TV disrupts sleep. Kids who watch more than two hours a day of TV are much more likely to have sleep problems. TV at night is no good, either. Nearly 30 percent of children ages 2 to 3 have a TV in their room, and those parents say it helps their kid sleep. But studies show that watching TV instead puts off bedtime, puts off falling asleep, makes baby more anxious about sleep, and shortens the time spent sleeping. A lack of sleep is bad for baby's long-term learning ability, not to mention mood and behavior the next day.

Other potential pitfalls

Preschoolers are particularly harmed by violent shows. That's likely because social norms haven't set in, kids at this age imitate so readily, and their social development is more malleable.

Kids are indiscriminate imitators. After watching one game of football, our 19-month-old (with more than a little encouragement from her dad) would raise both arms sky-high and squeal, "Touchy-down!" Cute. Less cute is that she would dive-bomb the floor and try to smack my head with hers. Between ages 2 and 5, kids can't readily differentiate fantasy from reality; they'll imitate "even the most unrealistic behavior patterns," as one study puts it. So are your kids watching things you want them to mimic?

Kids may not get the message. In one study, kids who watched educational TV became, over time, increasingly aggressive—not physically, but in their interpersonal relationships. (Like withholding a birthday-party invitation if the other child doesn't fulfill a request, or excluding a child from the group.)

These TV shows set up a conflict, usually based on interpersonal aggression, with a reconciliation at the end. But the kids, left to watch on their own, focused on the conflict and missed the moral of the story.

An episode of the show *Clifford the Big Red Dog*, for example, was intended to teach that friendship overcomes physical differences (one dog had three legs). But 90 percent of kindergarteners in a study couldn't identify the intended message.

How to watch TV: together, with you as interpreter

There is a way to mitigate the negatives and boost the positives of watching TV, studies show. Watch *with* your kids and talk about the show. Melissa Morgenlander, an educational consultant on kids' media and technology, offers advice on how to do that at coviewingconnection.com. First, she says, choose a kids' show you'll enjoy, too, and cuddle up with your kids. Then:

Is a character asking you questions? Then answer them! As dorky as you may feel about this, it really does make a difference if you talk to your TV when prompted. Play along! Count when they want you to count, say the magic word with them, sing the songs that you know.

Ask your own questions. This is one of the best ways to engage your kids. I like to do this while there is a lull in the action; occasionally I press pause on the remote. Ask open-ended questions like, "Why do you think he feels that way?" or "How did you know that was going to happen?"

Connect what you see to your child's life. Is Team Umizoomi at the aquarium? Recall with your child your trip to an aquarium. Is Alpha Pig on *Super Why!* feeling sad because his blocks were knocked over? Maybe your child once felt sad when his blocks were knocked over.

When the show is over, talk about it. As the credits are running, recap the show. Ask, "What was that about?" Review the major plot points. Find out your kids' favorite characters or parts of the show, and tell them yours. It's amazing how educational TV can be when a real-world grown-up reinforces the learning!

TRY THIS

Preschoolers get an average of four hours per day of screen time, twice the AAP's suggested maximum. Here are a few ways to cut back, from a study of kids aged 2½ to 5½:

- *Make a list, together with your kids, of things they can do besides watch TV.*
- *Together, read and discuss the children's book* The Berenstain Bears and Too Much TV.
- *Turn off the TV for a week. Help children make "No TV" signs for each TV set. Do the fun things on your list.*

Make screen time social

More than a million apps and games for your tablet or smartphone are labeled "educational." But that doesn't mean baby can learn from them.

Two guidelines are emerging:

1. The more responsive a technology is, the more a child can learn from it. If babies have to touch the screen in order to hear snippets of language, they learn more than they do from a passive experience.
2. The more social a technology is, the better. If two babies touch a screen together, for example, they learn twice as much as they do when they're flying solo.

Past age 2, children are more readily able to learn from screens (see page 140). But because other things in life—social interaction, exercise, play, talk—are so much more important for a child's healthy development, the American Academy of Pediatrics recommends less than two hours a day of total screen time (TVs, computers, cell phones, etc.).

Here are some ideas for mediating the screens in your child's life.

Set limits

Choose the content. Select a set of books, websites, games, or apps your children will be allowed to access. Look for ratings and reviews at Common Sense Media (commonsensemedia.org).

Set a daily time limit for screen time, based on prioritizing the most important things in your day. Exercise, play, and sleep are infinitely more important to a child's brain development than screen time, so make sure those are in order first.

Decide on a trade, such as three hours of active play for every hour of screen time. Kids ages 3 to 5 should be playing every hour throughout the day, for at least fifteen minutes at a time.

Give screen-time tokens, worth a certain number of minutes each, on weekends. Kids can cash them in after they've done their chores, played nicely, behaved well, or whatever you value. They decide whether to spend their tokens all at once or in chunks.

Save it for later. There's no evidence that not using computers will put your tot at a disadvantage. Older kids figure out the intuitive interfaces just as quickly. If you notice signs of addiction to a digital device, put the device away for a time.

Consider your own consumption. How much screen time will your kids consume as they grow older? The single most defining factor—more than the rules you set, or whether you watch as a family, or whether your kids have a TV in their room—is how much screen time *you* consume. Most families aren't worried about this. But if you're not OK with your kids spending the same amount of time you do with screens, work on changing your habits.

Enhance, don't replace, real-world learning

One thoughtful use of digital devices is as an extension of learning. I've used a map app on my phone to show baby where we are in the city as we ride the bus. One family who was raising caterpillars added to their experience by looking up time-lapse videos of a butterfly metamorphosis.

I love hearing what professionals steeped in this research actually do themselves at home. It's a little reminder to do what fits your values and works for your family.

Dimitri Christakis, a child-development expert and professor of pediatrics at the University of Washington and Seattle Children's Hospital, sums up his family's rules in the *Globe and Mail*:

> *I am a parent, and at home we do have our own rules—I think it's incumbent on parents to come up with their own rules. I also happen to think the Academy's recommended limit of two hours a day is excessive and it's not my personal recommendation.*
>
> *At home, we don't allow any recreational screen time during the week. By that, I mean mindless screen time—obviously how you define "mindless" is very subjective. For example, my son, who is now 15, composes electronic music on his computer. I don't consider that to be mindless recreation. We also don't include texting as part of screen time because, for better or worse, texting has essentially become the primary mode by which school-age children talk to each other today. We count that as "phone time," if you will.*

Sarina Natkin, Seattle parent coach and licensed social worker, says in an interview:

> *My family's rule is twenty minutes of screen time per weekday, a little more on weekends. That's partly because—after prioritizing sleep, playtime, homework, and dinner—there's not much time left in a day.*
>
> *It's also the rule that my daughters, ages 5 and 8, helped create. They decided whether to allot more time on weekends and no time during the week, or have daily tech time.*
>
> *They can't watch just anything. We have TiVO'd shows (no commercials), approved certain apps, and put selected websites into one folder that they can access.*

Percy and Amelia (4)

Play video games together

I have fond memories of my two sisters gathering around our Amiga computer, cheering me on while I played *Mike the Magic Dragon*. In the game, you had to jump and parachute between platforms, avoiding the bad guys, while collecting letters in the right order to spell computer terms like DOS and PRINTER. (Nerdy!) It was my favorite game, but it was always more fun when my sisters joined in.

If your kids love playing video games, play with them. Talk about the thrill of victory and the agony of defeat. Acknowledge the persistence it takes to improve and win.

Allow mistakes, discomfort, and boredom

It's hard to see your baby unhappy. But if you solve every problem for her, she can't learn how to solve problems herself.

Preparing your child for adulthood means helping her to see that she's capable of managing challenges. It involves giving her the skills to sit with discomfort, then move out of those feelings. It involves teaching her how to deal with hurt in healthy ways, rather than you taking hurts away.

Here are some strategies for developing baby's self-sufficiency:

Wait. When your toddler is trying to unscrew a lid, do you give him three seconds and then jump in? Take a minute, pull him onto your lap, and just wait. You might say, "Yep, twist left to open. Oops, if you twist left and right, the lid doesn't come off, huh?" If he gets close, say enthusiastically, "Almost!" You'll know when he's ready to give up. Ask, "Would you like help?" Then you might put your fingers over his and let him feel the motion of unscrewing the lid.

Show, don't just tell. When your 3-year-old declines to put on his coat, stand outside with him for a minute. "Why don't we check the weather. Brr! It's cold outside, isn't it! Let's put on our coats so we can be nice and warm."

Accept uncomfortable emotions. Label the feelings embarrassment, shame, guilt, and humility—not just the easy feelings. When *you* feel those things, say so. Allow your child to feel them, rather than being dismissive. Empathize. Don't jump to protect your child from tough feelings. Talk about ways to move through and past them.

Free up some free time. If you pack your children's day with activities and access to glowing screens, they don't have enough space to get bored—and then learn for themselves how to while away the time. When always-busy kids don't feel occupied, they grow agitated. They look to you to fill their time, because they haven't learned how to fill it themselves.

Boredom is a frustrating and restless state; the brain wants to get out of it. So, given practice, the brain will find constructive things to do: daydream, imagine, think through a problem, plan. That's why researchers say boredom can be central to learning and creativity. So next time you hear "I'm booored!" try some variation of, "Mmm. I'm reading right now. What are you going to do?"

Discipline

"Discipline" comes from words meaning "teaching" and "learning." The best teachers are both firm and kind. Our job is to teach lifelong skills: good communication, empathy, and respect for others—not "Do what I say, or else."

Phoebe (2½), Jenn & Paige (5)

Be firm but warm

A certain style of parenting tends to produce kids who are

- more self-reliant,
- more self-confident,
- more socially competent,
- less anxious, and
- less depressed.

These parents are attuned to and supportive of their children's needs, and they firmly but respectfully enforce their rules. Researcher Diana Baumrind of UC-Berkeley refers to this parenting style as "authoritative."

Study after study since the mid-1980s shows strong correlations between parenting style and a child's positive—or not-so-positive—social behavior.

That's not to say parenting style *guarantees* a certain type of child. Our influence on the way our kids turn out is limited. We're competing, of course, with genetics, peers, culture, and the other adults (nannies, teachers, grandparents, coaches) in our children's lives. Parents can claim maybe 20 percent to 50 percent of the influence, researchers say.

But we do what we can, right?

A CONTINUUM OF PARENTING STYLES

Authoritarian parents are firm but not warm. They have strict rules and expect their orders to be obeyed without explanation: "Why? Because I said so." Their children tend to be well behaved, but they are less able to develop critical self-regulation skills (see page 106). They also fall short in moral-reasoning abilities, because their sense of right and wrong is guided by external forces—threat of punishment—rather than internal principles.

Authoritative parents are both firm and warm. They are involved and responsive, with high expectations. They intentionally foster individuality and self-assertion. When they set rules, for example, they invite discussion about the parameters of those rules. When the rules are broken, they make sure there are consequences. They discipline to teach instead of punish.

Permissive parents are warm but not firm. They are nurturing and communicative, but also indulgent. They tend to avoid confrontation and are reluctant to discipline, so they don't enforce their rules. Their children tend to have high self-esteem but also are more impulsive, more likely to abuse drugs and alcohol, and more likely to get into trouble at school.

Uninvolved parents are neither firm nor warm. They provide for their children's basic needs but are otherwise disengaged. Their children are the most likely to be delinquent.

Claire (3 ½) and Michelle (24 weeks)

WHAT PARENTING STYLES SOUND LIKE

Authoritarian	Authoritative	Permissive
"Hey! Don't cut in line. Move out of the way; let that kid go first."	"You need to wait your turn, honey."	Watches child cut. Apologizes to other parent with a little laugh.
"We're leaving now." If kid keeps playing, picks him up and goes.	"In five minutes, it will be time to go." . . . "One more turn on the slide and then get your coat." If kid keeps playing, picks him up and goes.	"It's time to go now, OK?" If kid keeps playing, parent sits there.
"Stop and put your shoe back on."	"Good problem solving! Your shoe came off, but you figured out how to keep climbing."	"I think you should put your shoe back on?"
"Get over here. Apologize right now. Do that again and you'll be sorry."	"We don't hit when we're angry. What could you do instead? We can't stay here if you're going to hit people."	"If you hit someone again, we're going to leave. What did I tell you? Don't do that again. Do you want to leave? I asked you not to hit people. I said stop. Do you want to leave? Hit again and we'll leave."
"Sit down."	"Please sit down in your stroller. It would make Mommy very sad if you fell out and hurt yourself."	"Please sit down. It would be better if you sat down. OK, you can stand for just a little bit."
"You're still hungry? Sorry, you already had a snack. The rule is one."	"You're still hungry? OK, you can eat these grapes or one piece of cheese."	"You're still hungry? OK, eat whatever you want."

What's your parenting style?

Your parenting style will be influenced by your child's temperament, by your own temperament, by how *you* were parented, and by what other parents around you are doing. (And by whether your child just popped out of her room at bedtime for the third time or for the thirteenth time.)

It's easier to be authoritarian, to threaten or spank and be done with it. Being authoritative takes more time, effort, and patience. So give yourself room to mess up and try again next time, especially if you're not a patient person or you don't have authoritative parents as role models.

Choosing a certain parenting style, rather than reacting impulsively, may really take work. I find myself making small corrections every day. In the end, it's up to you and your partner to continually be aware of what you're doing, stop and think about it, and make the choice. You can also get support from a counselor, parent coach, or parent-education class.

Different kids need different parenting

Aim to be authoritative. But think of authoritative parenting as a spectrum. The style I just described works well for bold, assertive, or cooperative children. Difficult, impulsive, or defiant children need more firmness and restrictiveness—closer on the spectrum to an authoritarian style—to avoid becoming physically or interpersonally aggressive. Shy, anxious, or fearful children need very gentle guidance, closer to a permissive style.

Follow four rules about rules

Kids need boundaries, and rules are what provide those boundaries. These four guidelines will help you create effective family rules.

1. Make your rules clear and consistent

You must apply rules consistently for them to be effective over the long term. And we are talking long term, because you're going to be repeating these rules many, many, many, many times.

Sometimes this is easy. Telling my toddler not to touch the stove is something I do swiftly and with a tone of urgency, every time she gets close.

Sometimes I'm not so quick. For example, my toddler likes to stand on the dining table. Oh, she knows the rule. Even as she hoists a leg up, she shakes her head and says, "No climbing onna table." If I stop her every single time, that is much more effective than if I *almost* always stop her but occasionally laugh at the little tap dance she does up there. (Can you tell I've already messed this up?)

It's also easier to be consistent about a few rules that are very important to you, rather than trying to enforce twenty rules at once.

Easy or not, the fact remains: if you're inconsistent about applying the rule, your child will be confused about whether it's really a rule.

You'll have plenty of chances to practice as your kid tests a rule again and again to learn its relative importance, to establish the limits of his independence, to test your reaction—and maybe to try to get that laugh out of you one more time.

2. Give the reason for the rule

Your child will be far more likely to follow a rule if you add just one line: the explanation for it.

"Please close the screen door."

"Please close the screen door. We would be so sad if the cat ran away."

The second request sounds a lot more reasonable, right?

Say your child doesn't obey, and you enforce the rule via a consequence. Children who hear reasons for rules are able to make the connection between the rule and the misbehavior: "I shouldn't do that because [whatever reason you gave]." Over time, this thought process allows your child to incorporate the rule into her own set of values, consider other applications for the rule, and eventually comply with the rule even when no one is looking.

Children who don't hear reasons for rules can draw only one conclusion: "I shouldn't do that because I'll get in trouble." Their behavior ends up being guided by an external threat of punishment rather than by an internal set of morals. Strong morals—the personal beliefs we use to judge right and wrong—provide kids with an important set of tools for navigating the world as they grow up.

TRY THIS

How consistent are you really? Step back and consider, from your child's perspective, what message he might be getting from your actions—not just your words.

3. Help your child follow the rule

Like us—except far more often—kids forget things, get distracted, and make mistakes. Reminding your kids of your expectations and agreements helps them engage critical thought and offers them a chance to practice self-regulation.

Prompt your child just before an event where a rule usually gets broken; say, your child has trouble turning off the TV, or hits during playdates, or whines while shopping.

"What's our rule about begging for toys at the store? And what will happen if you break our rule?"

Notice the absence of bad behavior and praise it:

"You're playing really nicely. Great job."

"Thank you for sitting still. I know it's hard."

At the first hint of an infraction, repeat the prompt:

"What's our agreement?"

"What do you need to be doing right now?"

"Would you like to turn off the TV or would you like me to?"

If these fail, calmly go to your chosen consequence:

"You know the rule. We're leaving the store now. I'm hopeful that next time you'll make a different choice."

4. Set rules together

Have you ever had a boss who commanded your every move and didn't want to hear your input? It feels horrible. You practically want to rebel out of spite. It also sets up a power struggle: neither person wants to lose, and whoever does is bound to resent it.

Don't be that boss. Instead, involve your children in setting rules. It's important to do this when everyone is calm, not in the middle of some rule-breaking. The process makes your children feel respected, valued, and treated fairly. Plus, their good ideas might surprise you. Go team!

Set a time to talk. Say you notice that your child is spending more time than you'd like in front of the TV. You tell him so, and that at dinner you'll talk about creating some rules around TV time.

Frame the problem. Together with your child, list the priorities for the afternoon: homework, dinner, playing, reading, bedtime. "So," you say, "we have thirty minutes per day for TV." Get input: "Are there other things you'd like time to do each day that are important to you?"

Encourage input on those aspects where you can be flexible. For example: "When would you like to watch your thirty minutes of TV? Before dinner or after dinner?" "What are some ideas for consequences if you don't turn off the TV when I ask you to? What could we do so that I don't have to ask?"

State the rule you've agreed to. "OK, our agreement is that you can watch thirty minutes of TV after doing your homework. And that if you don't turn off the TV when the timer goes off, you'll lose tomorrow's minutes one by one."

Emotion first. Problem second.

"I want my mommy. I want my daddy," our friends' 2-year-old sobbed over and over.

We were babysitting him overnight, and he was distraught. We tried distracting him with stories. We sang songs. We tried food. Hugs. Walks. Long, reasoned explanations about how his parents were at a concert, but they were coming back tomorrow—promise. Nothing worked.

Later, we realized he couldn't even hear us: he'd flipped his lid.

That's what Dan Siegel, clinical professor of psychiatry at the UCLA School of Medicine, calls it. He has a great way of explaining how intense emotions shut down the brain's ability to reason:

1. **Hold up your hand.** You're going to make a model of the brain.
2. **Press your thumb to your palm.** The thumb is the limbic area, that ancient part of the brain that regulates emotions. It works in concert with the brain stem (the palm) to signal the rest of your body, including your heart rate and blood pressure.
3. **Wrap your fingers around your thumb.** Your fingers are the cortex, which allows thinking, reasoning, empathy, self-understanding, insight, and balance. Your fingertips are the prefrontal cortex, which is like a lid over the limbic area, keeping emotions in check.
4. **Now pop your fingers back up.** The prefrontal cortex has lost control, because in an emotional situation, the limbic area fires so strongly and repeatedly that it begins overriding the control of the prefrontal cortex. You're no longer able to reason or empathize or otherwise use that higher part of the brain. You've flipped your lid.

That's why it's completely pointless to reason with someone whose emotions are running high, like we tried to do with our friends' 2-year-old that night. And even though my husband and I know about emotion coaching, we'd forgotten about it in our increasing desperation: we'd flipped our lids, too.

This stuff takes practice.

You can see it coming

Now that you can visualize what's happening in the brain, you might start to recognize it: *I'm about to flip my lid,* or *I've already flipped; I need a break.* And you can see it happening in your kids, like when they throw a tantrum or hit.

"We often think that our child needs to learn a lesson here," says parent coach Sarina Natkin, "and we need to teach that lesson immediately."

But baby can't learn anything when he's flipped his lid. That's why, in the face of intense emotions, it's more productive to:

Acknowledge the emotions first. Label intense feelings (see next page) with empathy.

Deal with the underlying problem second (see page 166).

TRY THIS

Teach the hand model to your 5-year-old, and she might start to tell you when she needs a break. (And probably when you need one, too.)

Label intense emotions

Brain-imaging research shows that verbally naming an intense emotion calms you down. "Name it to tame it," as UCLA psychiatry professor Dan Siegel puts it.

When we babysat our friends' 2-year-old, and he started sobbing about wanting to go home, we tried all sorts of things. But we should have gone straight to the emotion, with empathy, for as long as it took to calm him down:

"Oh, sweetie. You want your mommy and daddy. You're feeling so sad right now. Yes, I know, that doesn't feel very good." We could have shown him the pictures of his parents on our wall, and helped him imagine their return. "I bet they'll give you big hugs. That will feel so good."

The next time we watched him, I just held him, rocked him and patted his back as he sobbed for his mommy and daddy. He didn't name his emotion, but he heard me gently do it for him. He calmed down in less than ten minutes—then fell asleep in my arms.

Naming and talking about your child's emotion also helps him to eventually be able to do it himself.

Children who can name their own feelings are able to reflect on their feelings, discuss them, decide how to deal with them, recognize feelings in others, and empathize. They tolerate frustration better and get into fewer fights, numerous studies show. They're healthier, less lonely, less impulsive, and more focused. They achieve more academically, too.

For you to be able to name your child's emotion, you need to do a couple things:

Be aware of feelings—your own and others'. Practice by naming your feelings as you go about your day: "I'm feeling anger." "That's frustration." Stating feelings as observations ("I notice I'm feeling sad"), rather than as character traits ("I'm sad"), gives you a little distance from them.

Be accepting of all feelings. Maybe your first response to your friends' 2-year-old would be, "You can go home when your parents get back, but for now, let's be happy and play." Or "Big boys don't cry." Or "Your parents aren't here! So quit crying." None of these responses acknowledge the validity of the emotion.

Being dismissive of feelings has roots in the way we were raised. But we can try not to pass that on to our children. Study after study shows the importance of accepting and addressing emotions, no matter how uncomfortable that may be.

Technically, some scientists would say emotions are just the brain's way of tagging an event as "very important." Abstractly, emotions just *are*. As you know, no amount of burying or judging or wishing can make them go away.

Might as well accept them.

Ways to help your child identify emotions

- Read stories where the characters deal with feelings. Talk about a time when your child felt that way.
- Put up pictures showing different emotions (pictures you took, or cut from magazines, or bought as a set). When your child is emotional, present the pictures: "Here's a sad baby. He's crying. Are you a sad baby, too?"
- Help your child reenact a distressing event using stuffed animals.
- Look for a day care or school that practices emotion coaching.

- With school-age children, create an "emotional thermometer" labeled calm, happy, frustrated, angry. Explain how emotions often grow in intensity. Occasionally ask where your child is on the thermometer, which helps her get used to checking in on her own.
- Do a "body check." "Your shoulders are hunched and your fists are clenched, so it looks like you're frustrated right now."

Practice now, while the stakes are low

Why start when kids are young? Because identifying your own emotions takes so much practice. You want your child to have this skill in place later in life, when the stakes are higher: for being excluded from the group, for that first heartbreak, for not making the team, for dealing with the stresses of college, for managing frustrations at the office, for making a marriage work.

Wolfie (10 months) & Boo

TRY THIS

Kids erupt over things that seem ridiculous to adults. But saying, "Oh, you're OK" is dismissive, and even more upsetting. You wouldn't want to hear that if you were angry, right? Acknowledging intense emotions usually calms kids enough for you to make your point:

"You're mad. You don't want to wear these socks. You're saying, 'No socks!' You need to wear socks because it's cold outside. But would you like to help me put them on?"

"Are you frustrated? I know, it's frustrating when we want something and we can't have it. We'll bring these berries with us. You can have some when it's snack time."

If your child gets angry when you label emotions, start with stating the facts and brainstorming some solutions. Identify the emotion afterward. "You want to wear the green shirt, but it's dirty. What are three things we could do about this? . . . You were really disappointed."

Teach instead of punish

I assumed it would be a few years before I'd have to think about disciplining my sweet little baby. Nope.

I had less than twelve months before she started doing things I'd just told her not to—and then grinning about it!

My painful introduction to this came during breastfeeding. My baby, apparently testing out her sharp new teeth, started clamping down and then pulling off. I tried showing her my tears. "That really hurts mama!" I said sadly. She had no empathy. I tried biting her shoulder. She screamed; I felt *horrible*. I tried brief time-outs: setting her down next to me on the bed and closing up shop. That didn't quite work, since she was usually still hungry.

Finally, I tried teaching her what *to* do. We were using sign language at the time (see page 62), so she knew the concept of "gentle," which is signed by softly brushing one hand against the back of the other. We also had played "Say aah!," taking turns opening our mouths wide.

So the next time I (reluctantly) went to nurse her, I said, "Gentle, please. No biting Mommy. When you're done, just open your mouth. Like this." If she did, I praised her up and down: "THANK YOU, sweetie! You opened your mouth. Good gentle!" If she bit me, I called a brief time-out. And it worked.

It's not enough to discourage the bad behavior, as I learned. You also have to replace it by teaching the behavior you do want.

I am learning this lesson again at the moment. At 20 months old, my toddler suddenly started slapping me. My instinct was to gasp in betrayal, grab her wrist, and command, "No hitting!" She'd slap me again.

What did work was to say, "We don't hit people. You can hit pillows, but not people." Or I'd lightly brush her arm and say, "Hands are for touching gently." She'd then try out the suggestion. "Oh, *thank* you!" I'd gush if she rubbed my arm. "Mommies love massages!" (Next, I might go for "Mommies love foot rubs!")

The goal of discipline

We discipline, of course, to teach our children what is acceptable and unacceptable behavior. Traditionally we think of punishment as the best way to accomplish that. We might yell, lecture, spank, issue commands, or make threats that we can't (or don't) follow through on. And kids may do what we want . . . in the short term.

≫

Meg, Grant (19 months) & David (3½)

But what we're modeling through this kind of behavior is how to deal with strong emotions by losing self-control, how to communicate disrespectfully, and that physical force is a way to solve problems. The lessons most of us hope to teach are the opposite: how to control impulses, how to be respectful, and how to solve problems without hurting others.

Authoritative parents strive to dispense consequences firmly, swiftly, and calmly. They try to see problems as an opportunity to problem solve, rather than punish.

If you decide to view discipline that way, your child is more likely to

- learn the communication, self-control, and problem-solving skills essential for a successful life;
- understand we can control our actions, even if we can't control our emotions; and
- avoid getting into a power struggle.

Consequences vs. punishment

Aren't consequences the same thing as punishment? Not quite. It took me a minute to wrap my mind around this.

Punishment is authoritarian in nature and often employs shame or force. The punishment tends not to relate directly to the misbehavior (taking away dessert, say, for slapping a sibling). Parents' underlying beliefs are that their children are worthy of respect only when they obey, and that children are motivated to do better only by the fear of punishment.

Consequences are focused on helping a child develop self-control and an internal understanding of the rules, while respecting the child. Consequences are directly related to the misbehavior (taking away dessert for flipping a spoonful of it at a sibling). The underlying belief is that children, with reflection and practice, want to do better.

Guess which is which:

1. "Don't you dare throw toys. Look what you've done! Go to your room and stay there until I say you can come out."
2. "Throwing toys breaks them. We can't play with toys if we're going to throw them. This toy is going in time-out for fifteen minutes."

Punishment is a less effective discipline strategy, studies show, because

- children from authoritarian homes don't fare as well as children from authoritative homes (see page 150);
- people who are shamed are less likely to take personal responsibility;
- humiliation can lead to rage; and
- when it's not directly related to the misbehavior, it isn't as effective at helping children develop morals.

Why don't kids just follow the rules?

At some point, kids know they shouldn't hit or shove or snatch away toys. If you ask them, they will tell you it's wrong. But in the heat of the moment, they hit, because the knowledge hasn't yet become second nature. Knowledge becomes second nature only through repeated action. Through repeated action, knowledge is passed from the prefrontal cortex, where we do our logical thinking, to the subcortical regions of the brain, where actions are automatic.

Kids need to repeat the *action*. That's why lecturing isn't very effective. ("How many times do I have to tell you . . . ?") We can help our kids practice a new skill by modeling the desired action or providing other hints and prompts— a strategy called "scaffolding." For example, in some classrooms, children are given a drawing of an ear to hold when they should be listening and a drawing of a mouth when it's their turn to talk.

A little empathy and a lot of patience never hurt, either.

TRY THIS

The Wheel of Choice

When your child gets angry and acts out, one goal is to help him understand that, while he can't choose his emotions, he can choose his behavior. Enter the Wheel of Choice. It's an illustrated pie chart you make with your child, borrowed from Positive Discipline in the Classroom by Jane Nelsen.

A Wheel of Choice might have options like "Tell them to stop," "Count to ten," "Tell them how I feel," "Walk away," "Punch a pillow," "Save for family meeting" (see page 134), and "Apologize." When your child gets upset, ask which option he'd like to use.

Ways to respond that teach instead of punish

WHEN YOUR CHILD HITS

Get down on your child's level, look her in the eyes, and say firmly but kindly: "It's not OK to hit, because it hurts people." Don't get into a long lecture.

Ask, "How do you think your friend is feeling right now?" If your child doesn't answer, ask the person who was hit, or describe what you see.

Replace the bad behavior with good: "It's not OK to hit people, but it is OK to _____." "I felt really angry when you hit me. I'd like us to find other ways to let Mommy know that you're mad."

Remind her of your rule: "If you hit someone again, we'll have to leave." Or go straight to the consequence.

If she hits again, immediately and calmly leave (as calmly as you can while she's throwing a tantrum). "OK, we are not being safe with our bodies, so we need to leave now."

During a calm time, decide on the consequences of continuing to hit, such as leaving a place. Make sure your child knows the rule (see page 154). Try to figure out the underlying cause of the hitting, and talk about how to address that need in other ways.

Excerpted with permission from "Help, My Preschooler Is Hitting," growparenting.com

WHEN YOUR CHILD TALKS BACK

Stand up for yourself, without being mean, and then move on.

"I don't like that kind of talk. We talk nicely to one another in our family. Instead of 'I hate this soup!' you could say, 'I'm not wild about this soup.'" (This was my mom's preferred phrase when we didn't like her cooking.)

"I don't like it when you call me that. You can be angry with me, but it's not okay to call me a name."

"I am not going to keep playing this if you keep saying mean things to me. It hurts my feelings. I'll go do something else."

"Please don't be rude to me. I am not talking rudely to you."

Last three examples from "What Should I Do if My Child Talks Back?" examiner.com

WHEN SIBLINGS SQUABBLE

One mom makes her boys do squats, facing each other and holding hands with arms crossed, while chanting, "I am in trouble because of you. You are in trouble because of me." By the end, the boys are usually laughing and hugging. Love it.

The Wheel of Choice (see previous page) is another good option.

Lying is actually a sign that your child's "theory of mind," the ability to guess others' thoughts and motivations, is developing properly. Children enter this stage around age 2. Children at this age also are incredibly imaginative, not entirely clear on what is real and what is imagined, and testing out the boundaries of fantasy vs. reality through storytelling. They say things they wish to be true. They claim things are the opposite of what you see in front of your eyes.

It's not useful to get upset about untruths at this stage, even though the lies seem to be insulting your intelligence: "I'm not drinking cranberry juice in the living room." Respond matter-of-factly: "Looks to me like you are. Please take the cup into the kitchen."

"I made the sky." "Mmm, the sky is lovely, isn't it? I love this shade of blue."

"The tiger did it." "Ah. I'd like you to help your tiger clean up this spill."

"It was the baby!" "I know you *wish* your sister did this, but I know it was you. Please help me put this plant back in the pot."

By age 4, children know the difference between telling the truth and lying—and they lie like crazy, once every two hours. Children lie to avoid punishment, to avoid feelings of guilt or shame, as a way to get something they want, to preserve their relationships . . . the same reasons adults lie.

When you catch them, let them know: "That was a lie. We don't lie in this family." Thank them when they tell the truth. "I know that was difficult. I admire the way you're willing to face the consequences," is one example Jane Nelsen gives in *Positive Discipline A–Z*. Storytelling can help, too. One study found that kids were more likely to tell the truth if an adult read *George Washington and the Cherry Tree* with them before asking them to fess up. (Reading *The Boy Who Cried Wolf* slightly increased lying.)

But first, avoid putting your kids in a tough position by

making statements . . .	instead of asking questions
"Looks like the painting has been splattered with sauce. Tell me about that."	"Who did this to my painting?!"
"I see you have one of your friend's toys. We'll need to take that back."	"Did you steal this toy?!"
"I saw you break the cabinet door. I need you to tell me when something like that happens, so we can fix it."	"Why didn't you tell me you broke the cabinet door?"
"I see you didn't clean your room / do your homework. What do you need to be able to start?"	"Did you clean your room / do your homework?"

Then move to a logical consequence. For example, have your child help you fix or clean up the broken item. Have your child tell the friend that she took the toy, and apologize.

Consider the consequences

"I'm turning this car around right now!" "That's it—no TV for a week!"
"Then you can forget your best friend's birthday party!"

Oops.

In blurting out a random punishment for misbehavior, have you just punished yourself, too? Are you suddenly on the hook to spend the afternoon with an angry child instead of kicking back with a magazine? Or, since you don't really want to follow through on certain threats, are you going to look for an out, thus undermining your word?

Two kinds of consequences can help you respond to misbehavior in a more considered way.

Be logical

"Logical consequences" are consequences that are directly related to the specific misbehavior. If your child throws a toy, a logical consequence is to take that toy away for fifteen minutes, rather than, say, cancelling tomorrow's playdate. If your child keeps tipping his chair back during dinner, you might take away the chair and make him stand for the rest of the meal, rather than giving him an early bedtime. Children learn more from consequences that are logical rather than illogical.

There are three types of logical consequences, and each one is best used in particular situations:

"You break it, you fix it"
When your child breaks something or makes a mess (intentionally or not)

Require that your child solve the problem she caused: wipe up a spill, help a playmate rebuild a knocked-over tower, comfort a hurt child.

Take away a privilege
When your child defies, tests, or forgets rules that you've already made clear

Take away a privilege that's directly related to the misbehavior. If your child only partially cleans her room, for example, you might sweep up anything left on the floor and put the stuff in "toy time-out" for a day. If your child draws in a book instead of on blank paper, you might take away the crayons.

Call a calm-down
When your child is disruptive and needs a way to regain self-control

See page 172 for details.

Let nature take its course

"Natural consequences" are those that follow from your child's choice, without effort on your part. For example, you ask your child to bring his backpack inside when it starts raining, and he doesn't, so his homework gets wet. Or she hits a playmate, and her friend no longer wants to play with her. Or your child is disruptive in a restaurant, causing you to feel embarrassed and causing other people to give nasty looks (both are worth pointing out to your child).

Natural consequences are effective only if you don't interfere with the lesson, either by piling on (lecturing or saying "I told you so"), or by bailing out your child (bringing her lunch to school if she forgot it yet again). Instead, be empathetic and supportive: "I understand that it's hard to go hungry." "I know you can handle this."

But a natural consequence is not a good choice if

- your child doesn't seem to care about the consequence, like cold hands from refusing to wear mittens;
- the consequence is too far off in the future, like cavities from not brushing his teeth; and
- if safety is an issue—your child's safety or someone else's.

I encountered one mom a little too devoted to the concept of natural consequences. We were at a play gym, and my toddler readied herself to swing from a low bar. Another girl was perched on the mat, her head just about where my daughter's feet would kick. "Move over so you don't kick the baby," I said. Her mom corrected me: "Natural consequences!" Mmm, let's not.

TRY THIS

Nip it in the bud

Sometimes a cue or two can rein your child back in, if you do it quickly enough, before the behavior escalates. You might

- *ignore a small misdeed: keep your posture and expression neutral, without eye contact;*
- *give a stern look;*
- *make a gesture ("Shh");*
- *say your child's name in that one tone your parents used;*
- *physically move closer to your child, a subtle show that you're paying attention; and*
- *give a reminder: "What should you be doing right now?" "What are our rules about using watercolors?"*

Plan ahead to avoid trouble

What's better than a pound of punishment? As many ounces of prevention as possible.

Set your kid up for success. A tired, hungry, cranky baby is much more likely to misbehave. Make sure your child has enough sleep and exercise. Have snacks on hand. Don't run errands close to nap time. If you attempt a longer stretch of shopping (trying it once may cure you of the desire), plan breaks in a place where your child can race around. Ease the transitions between activities; for example, say "Bye-bye, toys" when it's time to clean up and go.

Give smiles, hugs, and choices. Children seek control, because who wants their every move to be managed by someone else? And they seek the attention they need from you. Giving both control and attention in positive ways reduces the likelihood that children will seek them in negative ways.

Really be present with your child for a time each day. Create moments of positive attention, like a wink, smile, or hug. Notice and praise good behavior.

Offer small choices to give your child more control over his day, such as which shirt to wear, using this cup or that one, or which books to read. Even when there's no real choice, you can create one: "Would you like to put on your shoes, or would you like me to help you?"

Explain what's about to happen. Setting expectations is one of the most useful things my husband and I have gotten into the habit of doing with baby. "We're going to sit on the potty, and then we'll play with the blocks. First potty, then play." "This is our last bedtime story. After this story, I'm going to say good night and close the door . . . OK, that was our last story. Now I'm going to leave and close the door. Good night, beautiful baby."

Say yes instead of no. "Yes, it would be nice to . . ." "Yes, I wish we could . . ." "Yes, you can do X after we do Y." "Absolutely, we can do that tomorrow."

Think before you act—or, at least, after. You're going to get caught off guard by baby's misbehavior, and your first reaction may or may not be what you'd like. But later, when you're calm, take the time to plan out a better response. Your plan might not go perfectly, but hey, you'll have plenty of chances to practice it.

Call a calm-down for yourself. As soon as you realize you're upset, distance yourself from the situation by taking some deep breaths until you can calmly reengage.

Remember that you can't control someone else's behavior. This concept has circumvented a lot of frustration for me. Infants are so adoring and compliant that you're a little thrown when your toddler starts up with "*No*, mama! I don't *WANT* it!" The truth is, you can't make your child do anything. And your child doesn't want to do everything you ask just because *you're* asking. Realizing that I can't make baby wear a hat, sit on the potty, or eat more dinner reduces tension around those daily things.

You can only tell your kids what you expect of them, and how you will behave if they choose not to comply. "That noise bothers our neighbors below us. Please stop banging the toy on the floor, or I will take it away." "Get down from the table on the count of three, or I will help you." "OK, last chance for potty. If you stand up again, it's diaper time."

Take the long view. If only children learned self-discipline—or anything else—in just one sitting. We parents have at least twenty years to teach this stuff to our kids—and even then the brain isn't finished developing. So when your kid fails to clean his room for the tenth time, maybe it's OK to say, "I think we're both really tired right now. Tomorrow let's talk and come up with a plan for keeping your room clean."

DINNERTIME! WHAT'S TAKING YOU GUYS SO LONG?

Our toddler suddenly refused to sit in her high chair during meals. She wanted to sit in our laps, take one bite, and go play. Trying to get some food in her, we found ourselves kind of chasing her around with a forkful of dinner.

Stepping back, we came up with a plan. Instead of trying to get her in the high chair first, we sat down and started eating our dinner. When she came over, wanting to climb in our laps, we said amenably, "Mommy sits in her chair at dinnertime. Daddy sits in his chair. You sit in your chair." She would protest; we would repeat ourselves and turn back to eating. Soon, she would climb into her high chair.

After a week or two of this routine, with my husband also using it at breakfast, baby no longer protested. Then, to my surprise, one day a few weeks later, she took her plate from the kitchen, set it on the dining room table, moved her chair into place, climbed up into it, buckled herself in, and announced it was dinnertime—before we sat down ourselves.

Rock your routines

Every day, my husband wakes up at the same time, pushes the jogging stroller along the same route, feeds our baby oatmeal for breakfast, and makes a ham sandwich for lunch.

Me, I'm all over the place. I might go to bed at 10:00 p.m. or 2:00 a.m. I might get wrapped up in a project and forget to eat lunch. But I know babies thrive on routine, so I work hard to keep our baby's meals and naps on a regular schedule. Her babysitters come on the same days each week. She goes to bed at about the same time each night, because we don't plan outings that conflict.

Research shows we're on the right track. Routines help kids:

- plan and make predictions about the future, helping to develop executive function.
- feel independent, because they're able to do part of a task themselves after practicing it over and over.
- practice self-control (see page 106).

For babies, routine means creating structure with consistent meal times, sleep times, and bedtime routines. After age 3 or so, you can help your kids create and follow their own routines. A checklist is one good way to start.

The checklist

Create a morning checklist together, written or just illustrated, of everything the kids need to do before school.

List no more than seven tasks. A 3-year-old might have only a few: go potty, eat breakfast, get dressed. A 5-year-old's list would include more tasks: get dressed, make bed, make lunch, eat breakfast, brush teeth, and put on shoes, coat, and backpack. Prompt your child to come up with the items: "And what will you need for walking outside?"

As the kids get distracted during their morning routine, remind them: "Check the list." That's it. Instead of yelling, "Did you brush your teeth? I told you ten minutes ago to brush your teeth! Where are your shoes?!" you can simply say, as many times as is needed: "What do you need to be doing right now? Check the list."

Within a few weeks of practice, kids start checking the list on their own. Mornings, parents report, look a lot less like mutiny.

Call a calm-down, not a time-out

Typical time-outs are carried out so ineffectively, it's better to just rename them.

What parents usually do is threaten a time-out, lecture, threaten again, finally send their child away, angrily wrestle their child back into the time-out spot a few times, yell at them to be quiet if they sound like they're having fun in there, fret over them if they're crying, make their child apologize afterward, and wrap up with a lecture. In other words, a heck of a lot of attention.

The truly effective technique? Briefly *withdrawing* attention from your child's misbehavior.

You go first:

"I need to calm down. I'm going to read in my room for a few minutes."

"Time for a calm-down. I'm going to take deep breaths."

"We're not going to talk about this until we're both calm."

Calm-downs are used for stopping disruptive or defiant behavior. But think of them as positive, not punitive. Their purpose is to give your child—and you—a moment to stop and regain self-control.

When you're not in the heat of the moment, prepare

Figure out what calms your child. What should your child be doing during a calm-down? Not "thinking about what she just did." That's not gonna happen; emotions are running too high. Instead, she should do an activity that you know tends to calm her.

Together, brainstorm ideas. It could be taking deep breaths (a 2½-year-old or 3-year-old can do this), punching a pillow, jumping up and down, mashing playdough, asking for a hug, looking at a book, listening to soothing music, drawing, stretching, doing windmills or sit-ups or squats, staring out the window . . . Whatever works.

Create a Wheel of Choice. Write the ideas on a pie chart, illustrating each item with a drawing or photo. Role-play each one, suggests parent coach Sarina Natkin, so your child is clear about what they mean. Pretend to be mad, go over to the Wheel of Choice, pick an option, and do that thing. Kids usually find this hilarious.

Choose a calm-down space. This could be a corner of the house or a spot in your child's room—a place your child chooses for herself. Make it cozy. Make it a place your child wants to go even when it's not time to cool off.

How to call a calm-down

1. **Keep the conversation short and sweet.** "OK, time for a calm-down." Be matter-of-fact, not threatening or disrespectful.

   It's not necessary to send your child away. (The key is withdrawing attention from the misbehavior, not necessarily the child.) You might say, "Would you like to sit next to me while you calm down?" Or "Would you like to go to your calm-down space, or should I go to mine?" If your child won't choose, Natkin says, announce your own plan for calming down: "I'm going to ___." You might add, "I love you, but I'm too worked up to talk about this right now."

   In some cases, say nothing at all. If you've told your children you will ignore any whining, simply don't respond to a whine. If you've told your children you'll pull over the car whenever they argue in the backseat, simply pull over. As soon as the misbehavior stops (give it thirty seconds to make sure), carry on.

2. **Practice a calming technique.** This does three things: It models for your child how to calm down. It calms you down. And it withdraws your attention from your child's misbehavior.

   You could take deep breaths, sit down with a book or your phone (even if you're too worked up to concentrate at first), or pick something from your child's Wheel of Choice.

   Depending on the situation, you might do these alone, your child might do them alone, or you might do them together. Some parents ask if their children would like a hug first.

3. **Later, teach the lesson.** Once everyone is calm, or even that evening, talk with your child about both the misbehavior and the desired behavior. Ask questions in a nonjudgmental way: "What happened there?" "What can you do differently next time?" "What do we need to do to make this right?"

WHY TYPICAL TIME-OUTS DON'T WORK WELL

Your child is overwhelmed by an intense emotion, which is why she's flipped her lid (see page 157) and acted out. She needs to regain self-control. Sending her to her room as a punishment doesn't teach her how to calm down.

If your child does stay in time-out, she's likely sitting there burning with resentment, not learning how to calm herself. In the end, studies show, she will be more compliant with your commands. But compliance out of fear of punishment isn't a goal of authoritative parents.

A calm-down lets your child practice dealing with intense emotions. This eventually teaches her an alternative to the behavior that led to the calm-down. It teaches her that taking a break when you're worked up is a good thing, not a bad thing.

Ask, "Can you think of a better way?"

The best praise is focused on a child's effort, not the child's traits. The same is true of criticism.

In one study, kindergarteners were given a scenario: a teacher asks them to create a house out of Legos, and they forget to put in windows. Then the teacher and child role-play what happens next, using dolls and speaking for them. (Researchers sometimes use this approach because young children readily imagine and insert themselves into role-playing scenarios.) Playing the part of her doll, the teacher says, "The house has no windows," and gives one of the following three criticisms.

Person criticism: "I'm disappointed in you."

Outcome criticism: "That's not the right way to do it, because the blocks are not straightened up and are still messy."

Process criticism: "Maybe you could think of another way to do it."

Researchers, led by Melissa Kamins and Carol Dweck at Columbia University, then assessed the children's feelings of self-worth: the extent to which the children felt smart, good, nice, and competent. The children rated their mood, and rated the house as a product.

Criticizing character hurts self-worth, mood, persistence

Children given person criticism rated themselves lower in self-worth, had a more negative mood, were less persistent, and were more likely to view this one instance of less-than-stellar performance as a reflection of their character.

Children given process criticism had far more positive ratings in every category, while the ratings by children given outcome criticism landed somewhere in the middle.

The children were asked to keep role-playing: "What happens next?" The answers of the children given person criticism are a little bit heartbreaking: "She should cry and go to bed." "The teacher got mad and went home." "He should get a time-out."

The answers of the children given process criticism: "I can do it again better if I take my time." "I'll take it apart and put it together again with windows." "I would say it's not finished yet, then I could cut out squares from paper and paste them onto the house."

TRY THIS

Here are a few ways to criticize the process rather than the person:

- *"What do you think happened here?"*
- *"What should we do differently next time?"*
- *"Can you think of a better way to do it?"*

avid (3½) and Meg

Move

Our bodies and brains crave movement. But if it was tough to fit in a workout before baby, try after. So now is a good time to multitask. Lifting baby is exercise, right? Can you get places you need to go, but without the car?

Maribel & Honorio (5 weeks)

Rock, jiggle, and swing

Babies crave motion so much, they go through a phase of doing it themselves: bouncing, swaying, rocking, and sometimes (upsettingly) head banging.

As it turns out, having a good sense of balance and motion is associated with baby's learning ability. Who would guess?

Scientist Lise Eliot suggests thinking of it this way: our higher-level emotional and cognitive abilities are built on top of a foundation of our sensory and motor abilities.

The part of the body that controls balance and motion, the vestibular system, is found to be lacking among children with emotional problems, attention deficits, learning disabilities, language disorders, and autism.

Motion soothes
Researchers had parents soothe newborns 2 to 4 days old by either holding them or rocking, carrying, and jiggling. The second option worked better.

Playing spin the baby

Sitting in a swivel chair with an infant on their laps, researchers spun around and stopped abruptly, waiting for thirty seconds before spinning again. Babies were held in several positions, to affect the three semicircular ear canals: head tilted forward thirty degrees, side-lying on the right, and side-lying on the left. Researchers did this spinning routine twice a week for a month, ten spins in each position. And? Compared to controls, the babies who spun had better reflexes and were better at sitting, crawling, standing, and walking.

TRY THIS

"Row, Row, Row Your Boat"

Get into airplane position: lay on your back with your knees close to your chest.
Set baby tummy-down on your shins, facing you, and hold baby's hands.

Sing "Row, row, row your boat, gently down the stream . . ."
Raise and lower your feet to move baby up and down

"Merrily, merrily, merrily, merrily . . ."
  Swim baby's arms

"Life is but a dream!"
  Cup baby's shoulders, one in each hand. Lift your feet up, straightening your legs,
  so baby is upside down. Lower baby back to the ground to finish.

...sa, Jace (2) & Owen

Keep moving

Exercise does tremendous things for mind, body, and soul.

It boosts problem-solving skill, abstract-thinking ability, long-term memory, reasoning, attention, and more. It reduces anxiety, stress, and depression. How? Exercise

- increases oxygen to the brain,
- helps create and protect neurons,
- elevates a chemical called brain-derived neurotrophic factor (or BDNF) that knocks down a toxic stress hormone, and
- releases chemical messengers (norepinephrine, serotonin, dopamine) that act against mood disorders.

All sorts of things, it turns out, go haywire in the body when you're sedentary.

I thought a sedentary person was someone who lays on the couch all day, eating chips and watching TV. Turns out "sedentary" refers to almost all of us. If you sit for most of the day, like at the office, you're at higher risk for chronic disease—*even if you do a workout at some point*. Excessive sitting has such a detrimental effect on your metabolic rate that Mayo Clinic researcher James Levine calls it a "lethal activity."

Harvard evolutionary biologist Daniel Lieberman estimates that our hunter-gatherer ancestors walked five and a half to nine miles a day. The conditions that forged our brains often are the ones we still thrive in today.

You still want to get vigorous exercise (where you're breathing hard) totaling at least thirty minutes per day. But it's just as important to be moving, not sitting, throughout the day. If you're a stay-at-home parent, you'll probably be grateful for just a moment to sit down and rest. If not, think seriously about ways to wean yourself from your car, your sit-down desk, and your TV.

This concept goes for baby, too. Toddlers need to toddle. Older kids need at least an hour a day of an aerobic activity, like running, jump rope, basketball, swimming, or soccer. Get them moving for at least fifteen minutes of every hour.

THE RESEARCH

Using data from a huge multiyear study on aging, researchers looked at sixty-three thousand men ages 45–64 and found that those who sat more than four hours a day were "significantly more likely" to have been diagnosed with heart disease, cancer, diabetes, or high blood pressure than those who sat less than four hours a day.

TRY THIS

The most useful piece of advice I've gotten from my toddler's pediatrician so far is to make sure she gets enough exercise during the day. If I don't make the effort to get us out of the house—yes, some days that takes effort— I notice that baby gets cranky, has trouble napping, and races around in the evening as if to make up for it. One of the best cures for crankiness seems to be walking outside.

Ideas for exercise

Look for gyms and yoga studios that offer child care (this costs only $3–$5 per session where I live, in Seattle—so worth it). Hopefully a class will land just outside of nap time. If you're a stay-at-home parent, put every option into your calendar so that you know where you can go when the opportunity strikes.

Join a parent-and-baby workout class like Stroller Strides, Strollercize, Stroller Fit, Baby Boot Camp, yoga, or swimming.

Get a jogging stroller so that you can get outside on your own schedule (meaning, on baby's unpredictable schedule).

Find a workout buddy. Ideally, this is someone whose kid takes predictable naps that line up with your kid's naps. Or someone who is flexible enough that you can adjust the timing on the fly, because it's so hard to get out of the house on time with a baby at first. Or someone who can meet you before baby wakes up or while your partner feeds baby breakfast.

Do something you love. If the word "workout" makes you shudder, go hiking or dancing or anything else where breaking a sweat is just a bonus.

DO IT NOW

What will you do to get thirty minutes of vigorous exercise? Be specific about the days, times, and places.

Lisa & Jace (2)

Tracy & Geneva (23 months)

Ideas for movement

Leave the car at home. Yes, it takes more time to walk the forty minutes to the restaurant than to drive the ten minutes. Is that so bad? You gain time to talk with your lunch date, you feel more connected to your surroundings, and you feel great after your meal. Perhaps a grocery store or farmers' market is within walking distance. You could stuff your purchases in the jogging stroller. Or you could bike for your errands, putting items in a backpack or saddlebag, or tucked around your child in a bike trailer. Even if the place is five miles away, getting there by bicycle will take only thirty minutes or so. Hey, now you've gotten your thirty minutes of vigorous exercise.

The idea that movement is more important than speed definitely takes a shift in thinking. You could work on it incrementally, like walking or biking part of the way, and busing or driving the rest. Or you could make a dramatic change, like choosing a smaller house in a walkable neighborhood over a suburban house where it's impractical to walk or bike.

Are you thinking, "I couldn't do that"?

Take a minute to write out your concerns. Next to each one, brainstorm about what would remove that obstacle. For example, if biking seems impossible because "I don't know how I'd get there," resolve to check a few routes using the biking and bus options built into Google Maps, and begin imagining how it could work.

If it's "I don't like walking in this weather," resolve to buy the right gear, try it, and see if it's as horrible as you imagine. If one benefit of a suburban home is "a safe place for kids to play," your requirement of an urban home could be "on a quiet street near a park."

Dig into the why, and come up with the why not.

Stand at your desk. It's hard to get away from sitting eight hours a day if there's a chair at your desk. Fortunately, standing desks no longer seem weird. (Mine involves a laptop on a plastic storage bin, and an external monitor, but there are fancier options.) Treadmill desks aren't far behind; you can even buy them at Target. You walk slowly on them as you work.

Early adopters swear by treadmill desks. There's late-show host Jimmy Kimmel, weatherman Al Roker, and *New Yorker* staff writer Susan Orlean. Orlean told NPR that her afternoon work slump is gone, and she doesn't miss sitting: "The funny thing is that when I leave my office, it's not that I think, 'Oh my God, thank goodness I can finally go sit.' I find that I have more energy, and what often comes to mind is, 'Oh, I think I'll take the dog and go for a walk.'"

And there's "dworley" at instructables.com, who made me laugh: "[A]fter the initial adjustment period, during which walking was torture and standing was something I did for emergencies, I can now say that it's solely responsible for all the happiness I've ever had."

Choose the harder way. Take the stairs instead of the elevator, even if your office is twenty floors up. Carry baby in a wrap or hiking backpack instead of in a stroller. Run with the stroller instead of walk, even for a short stretch. Park as far away as possible. Our natural instinct is to choose the easy way, so you have to consciously override this.

Be a stay-at-home parent. You'll be on your feet all day! Stretching across the kitchen to cook and clean, bending down to pick up toys/baby/spills, wrestling baby into diapers and clothes, taking walks just to get out of the house . . . You'll still need thirty minutes of vigorous exercise, but in my experience, you sure won't be sitting.

$(\ \text{DO IT NOW}\ )$

What specific things will you do to keep from sitting for long stretches?

Slow down

Babies are slow. And babies are all-encompassing. The more present you are when you're with baby—leaving work at work, stashing digital distractions, and including baby in the day's tasks (even though they'll take longer)—the more you'll enjoy baby. Embrace baby pace.

Jace (2)

Be still

How often do we pause to just *be*?

Studies hint that people who meditate daily have

- more gray matter in parts of the brain associated with memory and learning, and less gray matter in parts of the brain associated with stress.
- more folds, and thus more neurons, in the cerebral cortex. The number of folds increases the more years one has been meditating, proving that brain growth is not on an irreversible decline after one's early 20s, as once thought.
- more empathy. When they hear the sounds of someone suffering, a part of the brain related to empathy reacts more strongly.
- longer attention spans.

The *New York Times* calls meditation "A bench press for the brain." That's because stillness—meditation—is challenging mental work.

Meditation isn't about sitting there with your eyes closed, trying to force your mind not to have thoughts. Instead, you continually bring your awareness back to the present moment, often by focusing your attention on the breath and letting random thoughts float away as they come up. Our minds really like to wander, so it takes work to stay in the present for more than a few seconds.

A mind that's better at focusing is also better at working memory (that's the ability to retain and use bits of information). In one study, researchers asked undergraduates to meditate for two weeks, and found that their working memory improved while their mind wandering decreased. On a GRE test, their average verbal-reasoning scores improved by 13 percent.

For kids, a walking meditation

Children have trouble sitting still for long (if you haven't noticed). But they can meditate by walking silently for five minutes at a time. In Montessori schools, children walk while holding a bell, trying not to let it ring.

After age 10, introduce the concept of sitting comfortably in a quiet place and focusing on the breath. Have your kids put a hand on their belly and notice how it feels to breathe deeply. Teach them to repeat a simple phrase, such as "Love," "Om," or "I am," said with each breath, which helps quiet the mind.

At Nataki Talibah Schoolhouse, a charter school in Detroit, students in fifth to eighth grades meditate by closing their eyes and silently repeating a mantra for ten minutes, twice a day. A study of the children found them to be happier, with higher self-esteem, better able to handle stress, and more socially skilled than children at another Detroit school who didn't meditate.

Something to keep in mind.

Be truly present in the moment

One powerful meditation practice is taking the time to really notice what you're experiencing at the moment.

It could be during a meal: chewing slowly, noticing the texture and tastes in your mouth, listening to the sound your teeth make, noticing what your tongue is doing and what happens in your throat as you swallow. It could be during a meeting: sensing how the muscles in your back and legs continually adjust as you're sitting. It could be during a hike: pausing in silence until you start to hear the chirps of distant birds, the rush of a stream, the wind rustling leaves, and the other subtle sounds of the forest.

Here's one exercise to help you get the idea, which might work with older kids, too. Find a partner, and sit comfortably close to each other. The first person asks, "What are you experiencing right now?"

The other person responds with whatever sensation or emotion or thought comes to mind. "The sound of birds outside." "Heat spreading across my chest." "A desire to hide."

The first person replies, "Thank you." As in, thank you for being vulnerable in this moment and sharing this thing with me.

Take a breath or two. Repeat the question. Go for five minutes, then switch roles.

Seattle teacher Brent Morton led a group of us through this exercise during a yoga retreat, and the experience stuck with me. A partner helps you stay focused on the meditation, because you know you'll need an answer to the upcoming question. Your answers get deeper as you go on, if you let them, and that vulnerability creates a connection with the other person. It also can be good practice in verbalizing your emotions (see page 158).

TRY THIS

Students (including 5-year-olds) in a traditional Tae Kwon Do class were directed to ask themselves three questions:

1. *Where am I?*

2. *What am I doing?*

3. *What should I be doing?*

The first question brings the student's focus to the present moment. The second question centers the student's mind on a specific, clear goal. The third question helps the student check in to see if his current actions will help him achieve the goal at hand.

I'm putting this tidbit in my back pocket, because these questions seem useful for a kid doing pretty much any activity. Heck, they seem useful for me.

TRY THIS

"Don't bother to compare" goes for parenting, too. We can be so judgmental of others' choices. The authors of I Was a Really Good Mom Before I Had Kids observe that this comes from a place of insecurity, a need to validate our own parenting choices. We're all doing the best we can, right? We need all the support and encouragement we can get. (If you're feeling the weight of high self-expectations, and you need a laugh, read that book.)

Don't bother to compare

My friend has figured out the correct answer to any baby-related news.

If you tell him your baby is now crawling/sitting/walking/talking/climbing/whatever, he will exclaim: "Al*ready?!?*" It feels good to hear that, right? We all want our babies to be at least a little bit north of average.

The reality: it's pointless to compare kids.

No two brains are the same

Children's brains don't go through developmental phases in the same way, at the same time, or in the same order. They may skip and then circle back to phases. They may repeat some. Even the phases themselves are in dispute. The brain is a mysterious thing.

And since both experiences and genetics wire our brains, it's impossible for any two brains to be the same—including those of identical twins.

Understand age-appropriate behavior

It's still helpful to know what most kids are capable of and when, so that your expectations aren't unrealistic.

Is your 3-month-old not sleeping through the night? Has your 18-month-old started slapping you? Does your 4-year-old seem even less willing to share than before? All normal. (You can sign up at babycenter.com for a weekly e-mail about what babies at a certain age are often up to.)

But the next time you're comparing notes with friends or forums, don't get overly worried or overly proud.

And the next time parents innocently fill you in on a milestone, make 'em feel good. "Al*ready?!?*"

Work part-time if you can (maybe less)

Among mothers who are married or have a household income of at least $50,000, 75 percent say that working part-time or not at all would be ideal.

Of mothers currently working full-time:	Of mothers currently not working:
44% would rather be working part-time	40% would rather be working part-time
9% would rather stay at home full-time	36% are happy staying at home full-time

Pew Research Center, March 2013

Moms are happier

Mothers working part-time through the preschool years report

- less depression than stay-at-home moms;
- better general health than stay-at-home moms;
- less social isolation, which affects mental health;
- greater ability to develop new skills, which also affects mental health;
- less work-family conflict, compared with women working full-time; and
- more sensitive parenting, compared with women working full-time or staying at home.

I can see how that would be.

Parenting for hours on end is exhausting mental work. Just from a brain perspective, it involves staying constantly alert, focusing attention and ignoring distractions, intuiting and responding to another person's needs one after the other, and acting with empathy and self-control.

Yet I know plenty of moms, myself included, who would feel guilty about arranging regular child care "just" for a break during the day. It's a recipe for overwhelm and stress, if not depression.

I'm in the 75 percent camp. I can tell I'm a better parent for working part-time. I feel more engaged with baby after a recharge. The work itself is intellectually stimulating. It's comforting to me to know that my skills and professional network won't go completely dormant during this stage of my life. I don't feel anxious about work-life balance, as I know I would if I were committed to a full-time job.

And I cherish the unhurried time I get to spend with my daughter. We might wait for a fly to land in the right spot so that we can capture it and let it "go home" outside. Or pause during a walk to examine water rushing down a drain. Or bike along Seattle's beautiful waterfront path instead of drive to a destination.

It feels like the good life.

Moms are equally happy

The statistics don't say, of course, that mothers who work full-time or stay at home are never happy. Once you look past preschool, the story shifts. At an equal rate, the Pew survey reports, women who work for pay and those who don't report being "very happy" with their lives: 36 percent for both groups. Being married is a stronger predictor of happiness than work status.

If you wanted to work part-time or less, could you afford it?

Families who make it work with less money are not necessarily "lucky." They're making sacrifices (whether voluntarily or, in the case of a job loss, not).

If you plan to live on less than two incomes, it helps to have saved money before baby arrives: an emergency fund, at the very least; maybe a babysitting fund; a paid-off mortgage if you really planned ahead. The main requirement, though, is a commitment to being frugal. Which actually can be rather nice.

Cooking meals from scratch is generally tastier, healthier, and an entertaining way to pass time with a toddler. Buying used instead of new means you won't be upset when baby's jacket gets permanently stained within twenty-four hours, or that toy goes missing, or your own clothes get peed on, or an item is never used at all. Washing cloth diapers and wipes turns out not to be that big a deal. Turning nights out on the town into potlucks and game nights, you find that you connect more deeply with your friends. Driving less, you connect more with your neighborhood. Even trading on the future, like not buying that house right now, or hitting pause on retirement savings for a few years, quickly feels worth it.

With deliberate planning, I can report, living on less works pretty well.

Tracy, Geneva (23 months) & Luke

Be more, do less

The little moments—the ones where you've chosen to be in the moment, rather than rushing or stressing or looking at your phone—those are the ones that you and your kids will cherish most.

Jace (2) & Owen

Paige (5)

Ziad, Sonia & Quentin (2)

Have you ever vacationed on an island and noticed on the first day that you were walking too fast?

It takes some time, but soon you relax into the pace of your new surroundings. You begin to tuck away your digital distractions, because they don't fit in. You start to smile at strangers who pass by, because they're smiling at you. Your strut slows to a saunter, and your words become drawn out. You let the day unfurl. Maybe you sit down next to the elderly man outside the café and chat for a bit. Maybe you lay down in a grassy park to watch the clouds float by and notice the sun warming your skin. It feels luxurious. It's so unlike a typical hurried and harried weekday at home.

An island vacation: that's what babies offer us, if we let them. Babies slow us down. My toddler and I can go for a walk to the park, five blocks away, and it'll take an hour to get there. She'll walk, hop, run, and twirl. She'll stop to fill her pocket, then mine, with rocks. She'll try to spin the wheels of the recycling bins lining the sidewalk, inspect gnarled tree roots, and watch water flowing into a drain. She'll call out the colors of parked cars, point to airplanes in delight, and shout with glee, "There goes the bus!" She'll laugh for seemingly no reason at all. Her joy at the world is contagious. If I try to shoehorn her into my pre-baby expectations of the speed of life, she's cranky and I'm tense. The more I embrace her pace, the nicer it feels to be together.

Baby invites you to slow down. This book is an appeal to accept that invitation.

In this book I've discussed:

- ways to truly connect with your partner, friends, and baby in the moments that make up a day.
- ways to teach instead of punish when baby tests you, an approach that requires taking the long view.
- the importance of embracing emotions, with empathy.
- ideas for moving, playing, and talking together.
- ideas for getting through the tough times with, I hope, plenty of laughs.

The philosophies and practical tips in these pages, research tells us, offer our best chance of raising happy and capable children: ones who are aware of and in control of their thoughts, behavior, and emotions.

≫

«

Knowing this stuff, though, doesn't make it easier to figure out why your newborn is still crying after an hour of walking, patting, and singing. It won't keep your heart from jumping when baby stumbles and falls. You'll still be baffled if one morning you have to persuade your toddler that, yes, she does want her dirty diaper changed. This book won't make it easier to clean beet juice off your light-colored carpet. Or to have patience when baby throws a fit over wearing pants. Or to get your sex life back. Or to (appear to) stay calm when your child leaves bite marks on someone else's child, lies to your face, or blurts out "I hate you!" for the first time.

Being a parent is hard work, no matter who you are. "Perfect" doesn't exist. Allow yourself many, many mistakes. Remember, this is the first time you've parented a 4-month-old, a 14-month-old, or a 4-year-old. And one bad day isn't going to define your child—or you—forever.

The other truth about parenting is that the tough moments quickly fade, because the good moments are so good. Baby smiles up at you or wraps her tiny fingers around one of yours, and your heart melts. Her round cheeks and tiny toes are eminently kissable. As soon as she's able, she puts your shoes on backward and clomps across the room. She runs to the door when you come home, squealing with happiness. She wants to do everything you do: eat your food, carry your bag, wear your clothes, say what you say, help you with your task. She makes connections between concepts that impress you. She snuggles into your lap on the couch for a story. She says the funniest things, and in the cutest voice. She gives you a kiss, or lays her head on your shoulder. When she sleeps, you've never seen any creature so beautiful.

Sometimes even in the middle of being upset, you can't help but smile at how darn cute your kid is. Just this afternoon I was incredibly frustrated that my toddler refused to stay in bed for a nap, and then she stood up on her bed and announced, "I need to get naked now." Babies are bizarre! Multiple times a day, you get to laugh, play, feel intense love, pride and joy, and be absolutely amazed. You may never feel so loved. It's like no other experience.

Everybody says this, but it's true: you're embarking on such a wondrous journey. I hope this book has given you and your baby a good start.

Tracy

www.zerotofive.net

Thank you!

This book would not have been possible without the work, love, and support of so many people. My husband, Luke Timmerman, took our daughter on "all-day daddy" outings when deadlines loomed. They even got stuck at Grandma and Grandpa's house, in Wisconsin, during a storm for six days—very helpful!

Photographer Betty Udesen went above and beyond, spending hours with families to capture the beautiful images throughout these pages. Editor Miles Wray gave insightful, thoughtful guidance that greatly improved the text. He also provided much-appreciated encouragement. Designer Nick Johnson worked with the utmost professionalism in creating a lively and inviting book and website. And he made me laugh.

Pear Press publisher Mark Pearson had two excellent ideas: let's publish this book, and let's finish working on it in Hawaii. Marty Westerman asked great questions. Carrie Wicks provided precision proofreading at the speed of light. Publicist Amy Hatch crafted a top-notch plan to get the word out.

Sarina Natkin has many titles: parent coach, licensed social worker, certified Gottman instructor, certified Positive Discipline trainer, cofounder of Grow Parenting, and perfect person to eat cupcakes with. My interviews with her were invaluable in shaping the discipline section.

A big thanks to researchers Adele Diamond, Ellen Winner, Samuel Mehr, Grover Whitehurst, Patricia Kuhl, and Megan McClelland, plus Sarina Natkin, for reviewing specific pages. Thanks to the newbie and veteran parents who rendered opinions of early drafts, including Kris Higginson, Melissa Allison, Ashley Sparks, Luke Timmerman, Kiersten Christensen, Trina Gorman, Nihat Sengul, Marina Cartier, and Carolina Toscano.

Betty and I are very grateful to the many friends, and several strangers, who agreed to be photographed with their children: Andréa with Arden; Kasia; Sarah and Heather with Opal and Zoey; Michelle and Tony with Claire and Nora; Myan; Percy and Maribel with Amelia and Honorio; Madeline and Greg with Claire; Ross and Jess with Naomi; Hope with Henry; Stacy with Mak; Abyaz and Melinda with Alianna, plus grandparents Mahmud and Parveen; Jerry and Karen with Miles; Sonia and Ziad with Zach and Quentin, plus friend Wheeler; Boo and Josh with Wolfie; Owen and Lisa with Jace; Meg with Grant and David; Jenn and Tom with Paige and Phoebe; pumpkin-patch kids Adam, Rose, Naomi, Grady and Nora; and Geneva's "twin," Maya. Thank you to Seattle Holistic Center and Music Together at Music Center of the Northwest for coordinating photo sessions with your classes.

A few others knowingly or unknowingly supported this book, too. Miles and I spent many an hour discussing edits in the café at Metropolitan Market in Lower Queen Anne. Nick and I revised page layouts at Roosters Cafe on Bainbridge Island (a refreshing bike ride and peaceful ferry ride away). Sutra Yoga kept me sane, especially classes by Matthew Coe, Rob and Melissa Lundsgaard, and Jenna Crouch. It's my home away from home. As soon as this book goes off to the printer, Trish Foss will need a spot in this list. I'm ready for a massage.

Thanks so much, everyone, for joining me on this journey!

Keep in touch

Join the Zero to Five community at **www.zerotofive.net**.
Share what's working (and not working) for you and connect with other parents.